HIDDEN TREASURES
FOR GOLDEN YEARS

HIDDEN TREASURES FOR GOLDEN YEARS

Louise L. Looney

All Scripture quotations are taken from the Holy Bible. The scripture references are as follows:

The Message (MSG) copyright 1993. Used by permission of NAV Press Publishing Group

The Bible in Today's English Version (TEV) copyright 1992 by the American Bible Society

The King James Version of the Bible (KJV)

The New Century Version (NCV) copyright 2005 Thomas Nelson, Inc. Used by Permission. All rights reserved.

The Holy Bible, New International Version (NIV) copyright 1975, 1978, 1984. International Bible Society. Used by permission of Zondervan Bible Publishers.

Holy Bible, New Living Translation (NLT) copyright 1996 used by permission of Tyndale House Publishers, Inc., Wheaton, Illinois 60189. All rights reserved.

Contemporary English Version (CEV) copyright 1995 by the American Bible Society. All rights reserved.

The New Revised Standard Version Bible (NRSV) copyright 1989 by the Division of Christian Education of the National Council of Churches of Christ.

The Amplified Bible (AMP). The Amplified Bible Old Testament, copyright 1965, 1987, by the Zondervan Corporation. The Amplified Bible New Testament, copyright 1954, 1958, 1987 by The Lockman Foundation. Used by permission.

ISBN 13: 978-1-936101-36-8

ISBN 10: 1-936101-36-X

CONTENTS

ACKNOWLEDGEMENTS

Thanks to my cheering section who urged me to finish this message. I'm grateful to Sam Lanford, who critiqued the manuscript and gave me great suggestions and feedback. The same gratitude is expressed to Joanne Hillman, who read the book and gave me meaningful input. Bette Lanahan came many times to help me deal with a rebellious computer, viruses, a cranky printer and prayers to spur me on. Janice Thompson picked me up when I became discouraged and took time from her jam-packed schedule to read the book and offer wise comments. I am grateful to Paul and Teri Looney for their words of wisdom. Thank-you, Sharon Tanner, for pulling many of the loose ends together. Thanks to Johnny Simmons and his wife Sue for their incredible commitment to get this message to everyone who might find hope in this phase of their lives. Countless others kept me on track.

Most of all, I'm grateful to my heavenly Father, who gently nudged me and sometimes pushed me to complete the work He assigned me. He taught me to depend on Him through prayer and gave me insightful and encouraging words to pass on to His aging children. I concluded—if He chose me, He can certainly choose you!

PREFACE

This book was birthed out of a burning desire to give hope and encouragement to God's older children. In searching through Scripture, I went to Ecclesiastes 12 and found Solomon's description of aging. While his dismal approach spoke of what happens to the outer man, God encouraged me to focus on the beautiful plan He has for the inner man.

It is my prayer that the reader's faith will grow stronger as he gains insight into the marvelous purpose Almighty God has designed for this season of life. May each reader discover hidden treasures revealed in His Word as he focuses on attitudes of the heart rather than outward appearance.

The book was written to inspire one to discover the beautiful inner spirit, trapped inside a gray cocoon, which will one day break free—released back to God. Then we will discover that we have been set free – free indeed!

Note:

Names that have been changed to protect a person's identity will be followed by an asterisk.

ECCLESIASTES TWELVE 12:1-13 (NIV).

Remember your Creator in the days of your youth,

Before the days of trouble come

And the years will approach when you will say,

"I have no pleasure in them"--

Before the sun and the moon and the stars grow dark,

And the clouds return after the rain;

When the keepers of the house tremble

And the strong men stoop,

When the grinders cease because they are few,

And those looking through the windows grow dim;

When the doors to the street are closed

And the sound of grinding fades;

When men rise up at the sound of birds,

But all their songs grow faint;

When men are afraid of heights

And of dangers in the streets;

When the almond tree blossoms

And the grasshopper drags himself along

And desire no longer is stirred.

Then man goes to his eternal home

And mourners go about the streets.

Remember him—before the silver cord is severed,

Or the golden bowl is broken;

Before the pitcher is shattered at the spring,

Or the wheel broken at the well,

And the dust returns to the ground it came from,

And the spirit returns to God who gave it.

"Meaningless! Meaningless!" says the Teacher, everything is meaningless!

. . . Now all has been heard;

Here is the conclusion of the matter;

Fear God and keep his commandments,

For this is the whole duty of man. . .

CHAPTER 1

SEARCHING FOR GOLD

"...and I am certain that God, who began the good work within you, will continue his work until it is finally finished on the day when Christ Jesus returns" (Phil. 1:6 NLT).

Seventy-five years old and counting. I'm scratching my head, wondering why they call these the golden years. Tell me one more time how valuable life is when the old body begins to grow weary and various parts start wearing out. Of course, I do have gold in my teeth. But no one seems interested in the silver in my hair or the gas on my stomach. Perhaps it's time to borrow a metal detector and go hunting for the gold, supposedly hidden somewhere between here and eternity.

The world declares I've reached a time when I'm 'over the hill'. That implies one can coast for the rest of the way, right? I listen carefully, but I can't hear God give me permission to lean back and take it easy.

§

Perhaps we should get the opinion of those who think we're of value. Grandchildren usually think we're special. My sister's

13

granddaughter climbed up in her lap and began to stroke her cheeks. "Marmee, I love your skin, I love your skin." I watched my sister smile as she accepted this lovely compliment. "Thank you honey, that's so sweet." The granddaughter slid off my sister's lap, ran across the room, turned around and giggled, "It's sooo loose." My sister's countenance fell and her self-image slithered down the drain. "Oh well."

Later, I went into the bathroom and stared in the mirror. I held out my arms and shook them. It was disgusting to see flab flopping back and forth under my upper arm. I looked at my face. It looked like a roadmap with trails of wrinkles connecting every village in the area. Reality hit further when I stepped out of the tub the next morning. I gasped at my reflection in the mirror. My old body consisted of organs that had moved south. Fully clothed, using camouflage techniques, it looks bad enough. Stark naked, it's sad. I decided to fulfill the Scripture that speaks of those who look in a mirror—then forget what they look like.

§

The impact of what others think of aging came when I attended a seminar with a beautiful young model. She spent hours in the bathroom every morning, attempting to look flawless and beautiful. It disturbed me—especially when I needed to get in the bathroom for a few minutes. I confronted her. "What will you do when you can no longer cover up every blemish or fine-line wrinkle?"

She looked at me in astonishment. "I can never imagine living past the age of thirty."

My heart sank. But on second thought, I too, am somewhat disturbed by outward evidences of age taking its toll. I need hope. It's high time to search the Scripture to see what God intends for the fall and winter seasons of life.

First, I went to the wisest man who ever lived, to see if he had answers. This led me to Ecclesiastes 12, where Solomon explained many things that confront those of us who are growing older. Great! The chapter is filled with one phrase after another which lists things that begin to go wrong with the passing of years. Thank you very much, Solomon! I can't tell you how much I need to be reminded of all the things that can fall apart in the process of aging.

I felt a gentle tap on my shoulder and a whisper caught my attention. "True, the things Solomon spoke of are real possibilities, but he only addressed issues concerning the physical body. Dig deeper and you'll find the exciting plans I have for a beautiful and vibrant new life I designed inside—where real beauty counts."

My heart beat faster. A tingle went up my spine as I realized the depth and breadth of the Scripture, "People judge by outward appearance, but the Lord looks at the heart" (1 Sam. 16:7 NLT). I choose to accept God's perspective.

With one surprise after another, the Word opened up vistas I'd never noticed before. As these surfaced, the importance of the outer body became less significant. Hope whistled a new tune in my heart. I realized that regardless of what happens to this shell of a body, God leads us to deep satisfaction and joy that will keep our hearts forever young.

The mystery regarding these invisible treasures for later years began to unfold. Tiny glimpses motivated me to study, to find what God would have me discover in these evening shadows of life.

Come—go with me on this exciting journey. Scan the pages of life as we look for those who've already successfully navigated these waters. Discover how God orchestrates a vast number of circumstances—to develop something of incredible beauty and worth.

I remembered events in the past and God's magnificent plan began to unfold. The lessons came from the young and the old, the simple and the brilliant. They challenged me to make a paradigm shift—from the focus on the outside to the inside—where God's secret transformation takes place. One particular scripture spurred me on. "And I am certain that God, who began the good work within you, will continue his work until it is finally finished on the day when Christ Jesus returns" (Phil. 1:6 NLT).

Scripture gave me the incentive to take each phrase of Ecclesiastes 12 and dissect it to find the greater good of what God concealed beneath the surface—down at the core—where seeds that produce new life are found. Each small discovery was bursting with wisdom as to how we make progress on the path that leads to His eternal kingdom.

THINGS TO CONSIDER

1. Have you ever wondered why we have to go through the aging process?

2. What virtues do you think God is most interested in developing as you age?

3. Do you believe God does have a purpose in all the things that happen as we grow older?

4. What aspects of aging discourage you?

5. Are you willing to search for meaning for this time of life?

6. Do you know others who remain upbeat and cheerful even as they age?

7. How much does attitude have to do with your happiness?

8. What do you think it means when Scripture says God looks at your heart?

9. Are you more concerned with what others think or what God thinks?

10. What percentage of time and money do you think people spend on trying to look younger?

CHAPTER 2

WHAT ARE WE TO REMEMBER?

"Remember your creator in the days
of your youth..." (Eccl. 12:1 NIV).

S olomon begins this passage with the discouraging an-
nouncement that we're to remember God when we're
young. Would this explain why some of us have missed it?
There are many things I wish I could undo or redo about the past,
but youth is long gone. If we failed to honor God when we were
young, can wisdom offer us hope at this late date?

God is our Redeemer and I'm convinced He's perfectly capable of redeeming our past. We have the opportunity now to spend
time building a deeper relationship with our Heavenly Father. At
any age, when we draw close to Him, we experience Him drawing near to us. He lifts us from our doldrums and surrounds us
with His love and compassion. Investing time in getting to know
God better now will overshadow any deficit of younger years.

It's great that no physical exertion is needed to deepen this
relationship with the Lord. In earlier years, I thought I had to
work my head off to stay on God's good side. I pictured myself
being suspended over a fiery caldron by a thread that He would

snip if I made one false move. As I studied the Word, however, I discovered it's about His grace rather than about all my effort.

GOD HAS ALWAYS HAD HIS EYE ON US

It thrilled me to learn God has been watching us all along, even before we were born. "You made all the delicate, inner parts of my body and knit me together in my mother's womb" (Psa.139:13 NLT). He's been there for each of us, when we didn't have a clue He was anywhere around. In eternity, we'll likely stand in awe as our past is unveiled. I believe we'll discover countless times when God protected us from danger or disaster.

We conclude that while we may not have been fully aware of our Creator in younger years, it's evident He remembered us. For instance, my parents told me that when I was three years old, I fell into a pond. I was unconscious when they pulled me out. By God's grace, they were able to revive me. It's quite clear, He watched over me then.

When I was ten years old, a conniving stranger urged me to go with him. I followed a short distance before the Lord swept caution over me and I turned back—while still in view of adults who stood nearby. I'm confident the Lord protected me. I praise God for the times He rescued me from danger.

§

One of the things I need to remember is child-like ways. Our Father intends for us to be child-like, but not childish. We once played a game in which a player drew a card and had to truthfully answer the question written on it. My husband picked a card that asked for an appropriate epitaph for his spouse's tombstone. "I think I'd put, 'She's the Oldest Little Girl I Know'." Hopefully he referred to child-like virtues of joy, forgiveness and trust. I'd like that.

DON'T FOCUS ON PAST REGRETS

Rather than remembering how God surrounded us in our childhood, some tend to remember the past with nostalgia. They're prone to drag out mementos from the closet in the form of photo albums, yellowed newspaper clippings, ribbons and trophies to hang on to snippets of bygone days. Careful! As we sort through these memories, we mustn't be disheartened and see them as evidence we've been relegated to a 'has-been' status.

It's highly unlikely our children will want to keep these reminders, and the Lord knows they won't sell in a garage sale. After we're gone, the memories of our accomplishments may be shoved to the back shelf of people's minds, and the mementos themselves—tossed out to be hauled away with the trash.

Satan no doubt picks up on our reminiscing and weasels in to spin his devious web by binding up our joy and immobilizing our hope for the days ahead. He permeates our thought life with memories of the way things 'used to be' or 'should have been' and attempts to trap us in a web of yester-years.

To foil the devil's schemes, we can commit to leave intangible, but beautiful memories for others—mental trophies of encouragement. What a delight to realize it's not too late to prepare a treasure chest of love and joy to bequeath to our heirs. We can construct a storehouse of fond memories. Go ahead.

Let the executors of our will discard the trophies and ribbons, because we'll have better keepsakes to leave with those whose lives we've touched.

THE RIGHT FOCUS ON BAD MEMORIES

Years ago at midnight, my niece was attacked, kidnapped and dragged into a vacant house where she was stabbed, raped and left to die. She survived by pretending to be dead so her assailant would stop stabbing her. Miraculously, after her attacker left, she crawled to a nearby house where they called for an ambulance to rush her to the hospital. Against all odds, she survived. Doctors told her parents, "There are five reasons she shouldn't have lived." Police confided, "She's likely to need counseling for the rest of her life."

God mercifully had a thoracic surgeon on duty the night of her tragedy. Days later when she stabilized, he told her, "You have a choice as to how you handle this assault. You can talk about it and work through it, or you can stuff it, and it will haunt you for the rest of your life." Thankfully, she chose to get beyond the trauma by talking and working through each gruesome detail.

As God would have it, He took that atrocity and wrapped it in a soft blanket of His mercy and she overcame the horrors of that ordeal. Our Lord watered her seed-like faith to help her formulate an attitude of dogged determination, to defeat the scheme of the evil one who was bent on her destruction. She resolutely declared, "That man ruined a portion of my life, but by God's grace he will not ruin the rest of it." She'll never forget the attack, but because God enfolded her in His care, the terrorizing experience no longer paralyzes her.

Wonder of wonders, she now works in an inner-city ministry that reaches out to former prisoners, indigents and men who have been involved in all sorts of crimes. No doubt some of them have been guilty of wicked and cruel assaults similar to what she experienced. Her dedicated outreach is to train and teach these men—so their lives can be redeemed. Some will become worthwhile citizens who will give to society rather than take from it.

Though we can't change our past, God can heal damaging blows from bad encounters. He encourages us to stand before Him and gradually open our clenched fists to release our hurts and fears to His care. How tenderly He touches each troubled spot until it loses its power to overwhelm us.

Our Lord can embrace those bad memories until they melt in His arms. He provides us with a gift of faith to trust Him with our pain. "The person who lives in a right relationship with God does it by embracing what God arranges for him" (Gal. 3:11 MSG). We ask for the ability to hold steady while He spreads a healing balm on wounds of the past.

§

The apostle Paul had a sordid track record of murdering and persecuting Christians—yet he announced, "One thing I do: Forgetting what is behind and straining toward what is ahead. . . ." (Phil. 3:13 NIV) Paul knew that if he kept dwelling on his past sins, they would block him from getting on with his new life in Christ. He trusted God to deal with the after-effects of what he'd done. Paul's repentance not only caused God to treat his sins like water under the bridge, but He washed them out to the depths of the sea, never to be remembered again. It's time for us to recall any bad memories and lift them up to ask God to th____ them overboard.

It's nonproductive to kick ourselves for past wrong-doings. For years, I struggled with guilt because I stole a nickel and cheated on some exams. I found Satan building a nest with those accusations, attempting to claim squatter's rights in my mind. That liar has no right to instant replays of everything we've done wrong. After we confess our sins, we can dismiss his accusations. Through forgiveness, Jesus makes it possible for our records to be wiped clean.

Every time Satan drags a bag of bad memories across our minds, we can refute his charges by telling him, "When you accuse me, I'm going to use it as a reminder to praise God, because He's made provisions for me to be forgiven for every bad thing I've ever done." Since the Father inhabits the praises of His people, this should send the tormentor scrambling!

The devil's attacks on our minds can show up in many different ways. He stirs up fear, worry, anger and self-pity to muddy our thinking, to get our minds off the Lord. He attempts to use our past to immobilize us.

§

When the economy went belly-up in the fall of 2008, I was shaken. We'd lost our retirement money in a bad investment and I'd quit working (for a salary) years before. My husband, my initial provider, was gone. When I grumbled and stewed about the situation, God whispered in my spirit, "Have I not taken good care of you?"

I thought back. When my husband died, a financial adviser told me, "You have enough money to last approximately five years. If you aren't careful, you'll be broke then." It has been twenty-three years. Time and again God has proven to be Jehovah Jireh, my Provider. "Thank you, Lord, You have taken care of me in exceptional ways." God continues to be with me—even when the money runs out before the month does. I've been rewarded with speaking engagements; people have come forward to finance my mission trips, and the list goes on.

REMEMBER THE GOOD

I went to Israel shortly after my husband died, during the Feast of Tabernacles. (Also called Sukkot or the Festival of Booths). This is a week when they celebrate the Jewish tradition of eating outdoors, under a shelter. They do this in remembrance of the forty years the Israelites lived in tents, when Moses led them through the wilderness to the land of Canaan.

A former US ambassador invited us to his home for dinner. The meal was served outside, under a canopy. Our host explained that during that week their families weren't to complain about anything. At mealtime, conversations were to be centered on the goodness of God and what He'd done in each of their lives. How delightful to sit around the table and share memories of our loving Father. The gratitude expressed in this experience tended to crowd out the negative cares of the world.

How comforting to wake up every morning, knowing God is the same as He's always been. He never changes. "Because of the Lord's great love, we are not consumed, for his compassions never fail. They are new every morning, great is your faithfulness. I say to myself, The Lord is my portion; therefore I will wait for him" (Lam. 3:22-24 NIV).

Since our lives are a mixed bag of hurry up and wait, we often experience impatience. God encourages us to wait for Him. The Holy Spirit can teach us the virtue of patience in the midst of a world that appears to be spinning out of control. He helps us to be sensitive, to know when to move forward and when to stand still.

It's Not too Late

If you failed to remember the Lord in the days of your youth, it's not too late. Read the parable of the men sent to work in the vineyard in Matthew 20:1-16. The men who came to work near the end of the day were paid a full day's wage. We find Jehovah is often the God of the eleventh hour. One of the men who died on the cross next to Jesus asked for and received forgiveness, only hours before he died.

One of my family members had been alienated from her mother for years. Her mom became seriously ill and she visited her in hospice care. Each asked the other for forgiveness and prayed for reconciliation. As her mother's life faded, this relative spent countless hours at her bedside. She read her scriptures, sang her mother's favorite songs, massaged her arms and legs with lotion and spoke lovingly to her. The nurse commented, "How peacefully your mother lies there during her final days." Her daughter became what God asked her to be—a minister of reconciliation.

I'm thankful we're not too old to crawl into the lap of our Abba Father—to thank and praise Him for being loving and trustworthy from the days of our youth. We'll remember to hang on to our Father while reaching out to lift others to Him.

THINGS TO CONSIDER

1. Think of times in your past when God was with you.

2. Is there some trauma or hurt from the past that still controls you? How do you manage trauma?

3. Do you spend too much time dwelling on the past?

4. What do you want people to remember about you after you're gone?

5. .Do you spend time thanking God for the things He's done for you?

6. Is there anyone from whom you need to seek reconciliation?

7. Do you continue to kick yourself for wrong things you've done?

8. How can you build good memories to leave with others?

9. Do you make an effort to recall pleasant things from the past?

10. Are you committed to get to know God better?

CHAPTER 3

TROUBLE CAME EARLY

"...before the days of trouble come..." (Eccl. 12:1 NIV).

I t would have been neat if we could've arrived on the scene before trouble. But it came charging in as soon as Adam and Eve fell in the Garden of Eden. Everything seems to have gotten off on the wrong foot soon after man stepped on planet earth.

Trouble announced itself in our family when Mom discovered she was pregnant with me, the eighth child, in the depths of the Great Depression. Neither she nor Dad turned cartwheels the day they realized I was on the way. My debut would offer no reason for celebration. However, when I was born, Mom wondrously gathered me under her wing like a mother hen—with all the rest of her chicks.

Trouble dogged my dad's heels almost everywhere he went. When I was only a few weeks old, he unhitched the team he used to pull a plow and one of the mules kicked him in the head, crushing the front of his skull. My brothers helped our mother get him into the car to rush him to the hospital. There, the doctor told Mom, "He'll not make it through the night."

Sleep deprived, Mom sat nervously drumming her fingers on her purse. My older brother Rex sat with her, gripping the arms of his chair and asked, "What are we going to do?" Mom pursed her lips like a tightened drawstring, "We pray." She not only prayed for his life but thanked God for answering her prayers when Dad survived. Time after time, with succeeding accidents, she opted for the same decision as he recovered time after time.

Trouble assaulted Dad with the loss of a finger and mangled others when his hand was thrown into the whirling blade of a circular saw. He lost an eye when an anhydrous ammonia coupling came loose and blew up in his face. He had broken bones and other injuries until he became so crippled he had to use two canes to get around. He fought with dogged determination to keep trouble from getting the upper hand.

He grew a vegetable garden to furnish food for his family and neighbors. We cringed when we learned he was hobbling out to the garden, sliding his hands down his canes until he fell to his knees and crawled up and down the rows—cultivating, planting, weeding and harvesting.

§

One year a deluge of rain came. "Oh no, Dad!" my brother cried out: "The water is rising in the bottom fields, ruining the crops. Is this rain ever gonna stop?"

"Son, never forget who sends the rain," Dad chided. "The Lord sends the rain on the just and the unjust."

Under the worst of circumstances, when others asked Dad how he was doing, he'd smile and nod his head in acceptance, "Thank you, I'm tolerable." Shortly before Dad died, he shook his head, "I just wish I'd known during the hardest of years that I wasn't supposed to do it alone." He found out late in life—when trouble was too high to climb over and too wide to go around—Jesus would always be there to go through it with him.

Handicaps failed to stifle his determination. He would not succumb to defeat. Job expressed it well in his book when he spoke of the frailty of humanity living in a world filled with trouble. When a calamity broadsided Dad, he prayed to God. Even now, I smile as I remember occasions when I'd hear his knees crack in church. I knew he was kneeling to pray.

At Dad's funeral, the minister said he'd watched Dad many times—standing, leaning on his canes, belting out hymns in a confident bass voice. "He reminded me of the Scripture describing the patriarch Jacob as he leaned on the top of his staff and worshipped God." He added, "But now, he enjoys the glorious new body God prepared for him."

DOES GOD REALLY HAVE ANSWERS?

The Valley of Achor, referred to in Joshua 7:26, means the Valley of Trouble. Dad was not the only one who found himself in that valley on multiple occasions. Many of you have been there too. However, the Lord never intended for any of us to list Achor as our permanent address. Murphy's Law, "Anything that can possibly go wrong, will go wrong" is not God's ultimatum.

Discouragement rests its case when God added, "I will make the Valley of Achor a door of hope" (Hos. 2:15 NIV). This shouts clearly, "God provides a doorway of hope each time we find ourselves trapped in a valley of trouble."

Doors are difficult to see if we're preoccupied by looking down and mulling over bad circumstances. It's time to ask the Lord for the courage to look up, to find that doorway of hope. It will surely open if we're willing to keep asking, knocking and seeking.

Clinging to a thread of hope is a challenge, especially when there's no obvious solution to our dilemma. However, we mustn't abandon hope, for it is Christ who encourages us to hold on—to take up our cross and follow Him. Hope lifts our heads and injects strength into our frail bodies.

Trouble attempts to distract us from being productive. It often comes wrapped in a package of confusion and frustration and tied up with a ribbon of self-pity. It arrives on our doorstep marked, *Special Delivery*.

Many see no possibility to adapt or adjust in order to stay on top of a situation:

> Too many mope,
>
> Trying to cope—
>
> Failing to look
>
> For the doorway of hope.

Trouble has been factored into our lives. It is not a matter of *if* trouble comes, but rather, *when* it comes. But we can refuse to allow difficulties to dominate our thought life. Trouble shouldn't be the main topic of our conversations. "I have told you these things so that in me you may have peace. In this world you will have trouble. But take heart! I have overcome the world" (Jn. 16:33 NIV).

There's no need to be caught off-guard. When trouble knocks at the door, we'll ask Jesus to go with us to meet it head on. Unlike a door-to-door salesman who occasionally comes to sell his wares— the enemy arrives regularly peddling a load of worrisome situations in an attempt to force his way in. We mustn't buy into his lies.

If we take yesterday's problems, add today's struggles and pile on the potential of things that could go wrong tomorrow, our emotions may well register *tilt*. The muscles of our character are strengthened when we exercise our God-given ability to conquer one problem at a time. "So don't worry about tomorrow, because tomorrow will have its own worries. Each day has enough troubles of its own" (Mt. 6:34 NCV).

LOOK AT PROBLEMS DIFFERENTLY

I met a beautiful woman who had been born to an unwed mother, but adopted into a family soon after her birth. That family loved her and gave her every advantage a biological child could want or need. They gave her voice lessons to develop a beautiful talent she later used for her livelihood and to sing praises to the Lord. In spite of this seemingly wonderful life, she still felt rejected and abandoned.

In a private conversation I said, "Danielle*, your birth parents may not have planned you, but God did. He fashioned the exact DNA from your birth parents for the unique purpose He had in mind for your life. I'd like to think at the moment you were conceived, the angels shouted across heaven, 'Danielle is on her way!'" The lady began to see her life from a different perspective. She realized she probably wouldn't have been given voice lessons, nor had many other advantages, if she'd remained

31

with her birth mother. What once she viewed as trouble, she now saw as an open door of opportunity—to fulfill the glorious plan God had for her.

COMMITTED TO GIVE EVERYTHING TO GOD

Though it's difficult to turn loose of troubles, we can remember the Scripture: "I know whom I have believed and am convinced that he is able to guard that which I have committed unto him against that day" (2 Tim. 1:12 NIV). We have a tendency to offer bits and pieces of our lives to God, picking and choosing what we're willing to release to Him. We need to be reminded, "If He only guards the things we've committed to Him, why cling to one iota of any troubling situation?" Worry is often the thread that ties us to our troubles.

A lady in my Bible class made a commitment to give everything to the Lord. The next week as she drove home from church, her car caught fire. She jumped out and stood there and watched it burn. She shook her head. "Lord, why are you burning up *your* car?" She told me, "Since I gave everything to Him, I suppose He can do whatever He wants with it." A heart-warming gesture followed when a friend offered to get her another car. It was better than the one that burned.

DON'T STAY TIED TO YOUR TROUBLES

You've likely heard the expression, "If you give a man enough rope, he's likely to hang himself." I've gotten so tangled up trying to understand my situation that both the rope and I became frazzled. Someone else advised, "When you get to the end of your rope, you should tie a knot and hang on." However, it seems it would be much better to hand the rope to God and allow him to pull us out of each mess—remembering He is our lifeline.

§

It's wonderful when we say we're ready to go with God. However, we'll never know we're totally committed until we've been tested. We're told our faith is like gold that has been refined by fire. "And these trials will prove that your faith is worth much more than gold. . ." (1 Pet. 1:7 CEV).

Each time we pass a test in life, we may sigh with relief and say with the little train engine, "I thought I could! I thought I could!" We might well envision Jesus in the background whispering, "I knew you could. I knew you could."

When I focus on my problems, I become distressed.

When I realize my inadequacies, I get depressed.

When I give my problems to God, I'm totally blessed.

§

Carey, my husband, walked in the door—his countenance reflecting discouragement. "You'll not believe what just happened. I went to close the deal on the sale of the farm and the potential buyer didn't even show up. That means we have no money to pay the huge balloon note that's due on our townhome next week."

He'd hardly gotten the words out of his mouth when the phone rang. "Yes, I understand, Mrs. Jones*", he said. "The note is due on Monday, but please let me tell you what just happened. We may need a few extra days." After he explained our plight,

33

he jerked the phone away from his ear as she shouted curses and threatened charges. Carey listened to her tirade for several minutes before he interrupted. "Mrs. Jones, until Monday, it's our problem. We may need a little extra time, but you can be sure we'll come up with the money as soon as possible."

Hanging up the phone, he shook his head: "She's been a bear to work with ever since owner-financing this townhome."

The next morning Carey got on the phone, scrambling to borrow money from every source he could think of—including getting loans on our two cars. By God's grace, he pulled the money together by the week-end. We went to the title company on Monday, with check in hand. After the deal closed, the people from the title company left the room. Carey raised his hand, "Wait, Mrs. Jones, I have something I need to talk to you about."

"What do you want?"

"Louise and I have been married for thirty-five years. During that period of time, we bought and sold twenty homes. In all those transactions, we've never dealt with anyone who has been as consistently rude as you have been."

"Wha…well, uh, I'm under a lot of pressure. My husband has been sick."

Carey stood gaunt and yellowed with jaundice because of cancer and liver failure. "It *is* difficult to be kind when you're under pressure and in pain, but that's no excuse for being rude."

Mrs. Jones sputtered and walked out.

Carey was dead within six weeks, but left a memory of holding steady in the midst of a heap of his own troubles. "Anyone signing up for the kingdom of God has to go through plenty of hard times" (Acts 14:22 MSG).

Trials seem to be a part of the exercise necessary in growing strong as a Christian. Aging presents many *opportunities* for us to mature as His children. We make decisions as to whether we accept what's happening to our bodies, or kick and scream with ugly complaints. The greatest consolation is that God will always see us through every change and challenge of growing older.

There are times when the heat gets turned up in order for us to be refined like gold. We can't always squirm out of this purifying process. "May God himself, the God of peace, sanctify you through and through" (1 Thess. 5:23 NIV). If Shadrach, Meshach, and Abednego came out of a fiery furnace unscathed, I'm sure we can too.

§

When we lived in Wyoming and Colorado, I often drove on ice and constantly repeated to myself, "Don't hit the brakes. Don't hit the brakes." Similar advice is appropriate when life's problems confront us: "Don't hit the panic button." Our own reasoning and resources are inadequate. We need the God of the universe to lead us safely across slippery places.

GIVE BIG TROUBLES AND LITTLE IRRITATIONS TO GOD

A friend came to my son Paul to tell him about a man he'd worked with who was in jail. "Could you go visit him?" he asked. "He wants to see you." Paul remembered Jesus encouraged us to visit those who are sick and in prison. He drove to the county jail on a hot day and stood in line for a long while, working his way to the window. When he reached the receptionist, she told him the prisoner was in building B. Paul walked over to the second building, only to discover a longer line than the first. Finally, at the desk they informed him that the man was in a third unit. Paul shrugged his shoulders, breathed a long sigh and went to building C. The line was not as long, but he was sweaty and tired. When he reached the window, they asked for his identification and he showed them his driver's license. The attendant looked at the records and said, "Your name is not on the visitor's list."

Paul took a deep breath and walked away. He reasoned, "Lord, I believe You nudged me to go to the jail. I went in obedience to you. I'm not responsible for the outcome and refuse to get upset about it." We commit to being obedient to God and then trust Him with the outcome.

The road mapped out for us sometimes feels like an obstacle course. Regardless of difficulties, we know we win as long as we follow the Lord. Our Father won't take us through anything that we can't emerge from, better and stronger. "No test or temptation that comes your way is beyond the course of what others have had to face. All you need to remember is that God will never let you be pushed past your limits. He'll always be there to help you come through it" (1 Cor. 10:13 MSG).

Though trouble comes early and stays late, we find comfort and hope here on planet earth, knowing our Magnificent Father gives us the ability not only to hold steady, but to grow stronger in an overcoming walk.

THINGS TO CONSIDER

1. Do you make excuses for the way you act?

2. How do you react to small irritations?

3. Do you believe God offers a doorway of hope in each troubling circumstance?

4. Does trouble distract you from your focus?

5. Do you believe God made you the way you are for a special purpose?

6. How can God go through your troubles with you?

7. Are you willing to commit everything to God?

8. Can you think of any good that either has or can come from trouble you've gone through?

9. Do your feelings or circumstances give you an excuse for a bad attitude?

10. Do you come through struggles stronger or weaker than you were before?

CHAPTER 4

EYESIGHT BEGINS TO FADE

"...the sun and the light and the moon
and the stars grow dark..." (Eccl. 12:1 NIV).

Those light fixtures God placed in the sky burn as brightly as ever, but poor vision partially blocks them from our view. Over time, it's our eyesight that fades rather than the light from heavenly bodies. Many of us don't have the clarity of vision we'd like.

Perhaps you've had the same difficulties I experienced in my forties. I began to push the book farther and farther away. Was osteoporosis causing my arms to shrink, along with my height? The truth smacked me in the face. My eyes were the source of the problem. Thankfully, I found an interesting Scripture: "Surely the arm of the Lord is not too short" (Isa. 59:1 NIV). "Lord, would You please hold the book for me?"

No doubt there are others of you who've gone from single-vision glasses to bifocals—then trifocals. It's 'glasses on, glasses off,' squinting to focus. There's another problem surfacing along with that—lost glasses. I cringe when I find them on top of my head. I also attempt to pick spots out of the air as they float across my field of vision. I'm also thankful for the magnifying glass on the desk, which enables me to read small print.

I wasn't pleased when my ophthalmologist told me, "I'll no longer be able to totally correct your vision."

"Why?"

"It's your age. Besides that, you have a wrinkled retina."

Oh, my word! My eyeballs are getting wrinkled, too! They must be crinkling up along with my skin. Since my flesh is beginning to look like crepe, perhaps I should change my name to Myrtle, and everyone could just call me, 'Crepe Myrtle'. One consolation is that as our eyesight gets worse, perhaps we won't notice the shape of our bodies!

Solomon suggests age brings the curse of failing eyesight. We face that reality when it becomes difficult to read street signs and we can't find our way around. This frustrating malady shows up in poor night vision, glaucoma, macular degeneration, cataracts and overall poor vision. Enough said—you get the picture—though you may not be able to see it well!

God placed much emphasis on light. At the dawn of creation, the Creator shouted and light exploded throughout the universe, banishing the darkness. He called for light and it streamed across the heavens and lit up the skies. The sun brightened the day in order for us to find our way around. He provided the night with soft moonlight, surrounded by a starry host, to set the tone for love and rest. Darkness moves out of the way when light comes shining through.

Light enables us to enjoy beautiful sunsets, waterfalls, lakes, flowers and trees. It seems ironic. Now that we have the time to stop and take in their beauty, we can't see and enjoy these as we once did. How true, we often don't appreciate a gift until it's gone.

KEEP YOUR EYES OPEN

When I was six, our parents sent my older brother Rex to take the milk and eggs to town to sell. Our older brother Don bet him he couldn't drive to the bridge, a half mile away, with his eyes closed. Don promised he'd whistle if Rex started to drive off the road. Rex took the dare, but didn't hear Don whistle—so he careened into a ditch, turning the car on its side. My brother Sam and I were in the back seat and ended up being covered with milk and broken eggs. This experience taught me not to drive with my eyes closed! Later, I realized I shouldn't risk closing my spiritual eyes either, because I'm likely to get off God's path. I don't want to end up with spiritual 'egg' on my face!

§

We have to choose to walk in the light. My son, Chip, rented the movie *Nanny McPhee* for his family to watch. A few days afterward Belle, his four-year-old, threw a walleyed fit. Chip took her on his lap and told her that her behavior was unacceptable. He calmed her a bit and asked, "Belle, do you remember the movie we just watched?"

"Yeess."

"You know how terrible those children acted and no one wanted to be around them?"

"Uh huh."

"You don't want to be like that, do you?"

"Nooo."

"Then what do you think you should do about it?"

She wailed, "Not watch the movie!" That was humorous, but it's tragic for those of us who stubbornly refuse to look at the lessons God has designed to teach godly virtues.

LESSONS TAUGHT GRAPHICALLY

One night in a home Bible study, we were handed scriptures relating to light. In the middle of our discussion, there was a power failure and all the lights in the neighborhood went out. Our host lit a number of candles in the room in order to continue the study. After about ten minutes, the lights flashed on and revealed the next Scripture: "But if we are living in the light as God is in the light, then we have fellowship with one another, and the blood of Jesus, his Son, cleanses us from all sin" (1 Jn. 1:7 NLT). Goose bumps popped up as we got the message—God, in an amazing way, illustrated how He wants us to live in His Light. He illuminates the need for us to love and support others in meaningful relationships.

It's easy to shine and have a wonderful attitude, with love for almost everyone, as long as there's no one else around! But just as soon as people come tromping in and say and do irritating things, our light may flicker and grow dim. When this happens, it should be a reminder to repent, plug in to our power source and get recharged. The Father commissions us as sons and daughters to be a light—even when we're challenged by others' dark actions and attitudes.

41

FOLLOW THE STAR

The Father brought forth the Light shining through His S O N, to drive back the darkness—where the evil one lurks. Jesus proclaimed himself as the Bright and Morning Star. When we follow this Star, as the wise men did, it still leads to the Messiah. Jesus addressed his followers, "I am the world's Light. No one who follows me stumbles around in the darkness. I provide plenty of light to live in" (Jn. 8:12 MSG). How exciting! We can scrub clean the windows of our hearts in order for His incredible light to shine through and guide us during difficult times.

We've been promised to experience more glorious scenes than we've found in nature. Gorgeous worldly beauty appears only for a moment before it vanishes or we pass it by. We only retain vague memories of what we see by attempting to paint mental pictures of each phenomenon.

Godly insight reveals the matchless beauty of His promises. These promises become more vivid and breathtaking as we uncover their deeper meaning. He shines on us with all His glory. Our anticipation of some day living in the beauty of His presence makes every day brighter.

God positioned His Bright and Morning Star as a compass, to guide us. During the dark and difficult times of our lives, we carefully follow that Star until the day dawns—when we can walk in the full light of the Son. This Morning Star creates a glow in our hearts, illuminated by hope. Jesus is ready to take us by the hand and lead us with insight, even when our physical eyesight begins to fail.

Listen more closely. In the midst of all this, we may hear a symphony of praise rising up to glorify His name.

DON'T BE AFRAID OF THE LIGHT

An old house we moved into was infested with cockroaches. Before exterminators came, we'd go into the kitchen at night and turn on the light and see those despicable bugs scampering everywhere—looking for a place to hide.

The light of God's Word exposes the dark areas of sin, but there's no need for us to run from the Light. God designed the Light to reveal our sins so He can clean us up, leaving no dark smudges to stain our character.

Spiritual Light makes our way clear. We don't have to continue to stumble around with a lack of insight. When we follow His guidance, we move ahead with confidence—walking along the perfect path He laid out for us.

Here on earth, we have the lights God created in the beginning. In heaven, His glory will be the Light and Jesus will be the Lamp. He wants those of us who are His children to be spiritual lights here on earth. We act as solar powered energy, absorbing His light in every cell of our body, until we glisten from the inside out. "And so we are transfigured much like the Messiah, our lives gradually becoming brighter and more beautiful as God enters our lives and we become like him" (2 Cor. 3:17 MSG). We can sing with Debby Boone the song she made popular— *You Light up My Life*. We take pleasure in lighting up someone else's day with Godly insight.

The Light of His truth leads us to new horizons—in spite of failing physical eyesight. God gives us spiritual insight, so we radiate with Christ-likeness. We open our eyes wide in wonder and expectation as He fills us with light.

At the end of the age, when the world begins to implode, we can count on God's glorious light to *explode*. I envision God sending out His angels, to gather those of us who have been His little fireflies, to usher us home, into His eternal Light. Our light may flicker like that of a firefly—sometimes on, sometimes off—but hopefully, it is becoming consistently brighter. "The way of the righteous is like the first gleam of dawn, which shines ever brighter until the full light of day" (Prov. 4:18 NLT). We shouldn't be surprised when others observe our whole countenance beginning to light up. Even dim eyes can begin to sparkle.

Remember, as eyesight begins to fail, it's time to search for INSIGHT. There's no age limit to become a brighter light than we've dared to believe, to lead others to the Father of Light. This is a strong admonition to keep on shining!

THINGS TO CONSIDER

1. How is spiritual light related to guidance?

2. How can God's light shine through you as an example to those around you?

3. Do you blame others or circumstances for the way you act?

4. What does it mean to have insight?

5. How do you go about improving your insight?

5. Think of someone in your life that has been a light for you.

6. How can you light up the lives of others?

7. Is there any area of your life where your influence is not as it should be?

8. Are you paying attention to what God may want to teach you in this period of life?

9. How can the light of your influence grow brighter as you grow older?

CHAPTER 5

CLOUDY VISION AND DARK CIRCUMSTANCES

"…and the clouds return after the rain…" (Eccl. 12:2 NIV).

It seems strange that the wise old king would say clouds come *after* the rain. Typically, we experience clouds rolling in before the first sprinkle. Since his previous statement likely refers to dimming eyesight, it's possible this phrase is in reference to cataracts that often cloud the vision as we grow older.

When I had my eyes checked, my doctor told me a cataract in my left eye had reduced my corrected vision to 20/70. He gave me the option of surgery now, or waiting. "Let's do it," I exclaimed, " Not only will I be thrilled with better vision, but so will all those who've trailed behind me when I've slowed to five miles an hour in an attempt to read street signs."

Psychological Damage Comes After a Storm

Let's consider psychological clouds. After life rains on our parade, dark emotional clouds coming rolling in. As disappointment punches holes in our reservoir of peace and joy, it drains the serotonin or good feelings from our brains. It is then that dark

46

clouds close in—heavy with the dirty 'D's: Despair, Despondency, Discouragement and Depression. They are thundering signals that we need to ask God to *reign* over our stormy encounters. Age has afforded a broad span of time for psychological attacks. If we let them stack up, they can become a frightening storm.

We've seen drawings of dark clouds hanging over the heads of comic strip characters. The stance of these cartoon figures is one of defeat—bent over with gloomy facial expressions and ominous clouds accompanying them everywhere they go.

Memories of bad experiences call us to battle. We can fight dismal reruns by refusing to replay them, finding instead something to distract us. Joy can play a big part in defeating unpleasant memories. My funny bone is usually tickled by watching some of the oldies, but goodies—reruns of comedy episodes—from slapstick to comic relief. Joy can be like helium, playfully lifting us above dark clouds.

§

I'd had a rough week. One upsetting thing after another hammered away at my peace of mind. Contentment was sucked down the drain. There'd been major computer problems, financial setbacks and an accident. Going with my usual response, I called Betty on her cell phone to ask her to pray for me. She didn't answer, so I left a message suggesting I needed prayer. She dropped by the house a few hours later. I asked if she got my message, and she said, "No, but I felt I needed to come by." We prayed before she went on her way. My clouded spirit began to lift.

That evening I got a phone call from a young man. "My name is not Betty, but I got your message on my cell phone this

47

morning. I wanted you to know, I've been praying for you all day. Call me any time." I swallowed hard, thanked him and hung up the phone. Had I dialed a wrong number? I don't think so.

We do have options as to how we handle our struggles. I guard against the temptation to pace the floor and wring my hands when I'm faced with difficulties. I've found stress offers an open invitation for self-pity to sit on my shoulder and whisper, "Oh, you poor thing".

Circumstances spell defeat when I allow negative emotions to come puffing in and snuff out glimmers of hope. When clouds of gloom press in, they become like fog, blocking the vision of the Son. They interfere with making rational choices. It's hard to pray when we're upset. That's why we need a back-up of at least one other person to pray with and for us. "So speak encouraging words to one another. Build up hope so you'll be together on this, no one left out, no one left behind" (1 Thess. 5:9 MSG).

For years, my husband Carey, kept a worn slip of paper in his billfold that read, "It seems that he was right who said, 'Life is what you make it. It isn't so much what happens, but the way in which you take it.'" We pray the Holy Spirit will send a gentle breeze of hope and joy to scatter dark thoughts, permitting us to make good decisions and handle life in a godly way.

ENCOUNTERING GRIEF AS DARK CLOUDS ROLL IN

A young mother named Teresa attended a retreat. Her life had become immobilized with grief because pneumococcal meningitis had taken the life of her little six-year-old daughter.

48

At the retreat I asked participants to take miscellaneous materials I'd laid out and make a collage that represented their life. Tears rolled down Teresa's cheeks as she worked on her project. She formed clouds of cotton puffs and drew giant raindrops falling on a field of brilliant flowers. When she explained her poster to the group, she told us the raindrops represented her tears for the little girl she'd lost. The flowers represented something beautiful she hoped would come from her pain. Our empathy and love surrounded her as we grieved the loss of her precious child. God encourages us to help others carry their burdens.

God gave us tears. He never intended that we squelch our emotions, but rather, allow them to be an outlet for grief. Tears may well be a process of cleansing the soul, but they should never drown our hope.

Teresa experienced some healing as she constructed a poster symbolically expressing her grief. She discovered she was not alone. She made a decision—she'd not allow grief to keep her from expressing love to her other three girls—beautiful little flowers, thirsty for loving care. Her pain was very deep but she would not shut herself away from the world by permitting her sorrow to consume her.

Now, several years later, her daughters are blossoming into fine young ladies because of her decision. In our losses, we're not only responsible for our own emotions and grief, but it is a time to take a close look at how our responses affect those around us.

Since we are a part of the family of God, we feel free to show compassion to our brothers and sisters in Christ. Jesus wept with Mary and Martha as they grieved over the death of their brother

Lazarus, even though He knew that He would raise him from the dead. We are rewarded when we sow seeds of loving concern for others. "Those who sow in tears will reap with songs of joy. He who goes out weeping, carrying seeds to sow, will return with songs of joy, carrying sheaves with him" (Psa. 126:6 NIV).

§

When bad things happen, we can ask God to breathe on dying embers of hope—to fan them into flame again. It's encouraging to know that God can strengthen us in our trials so that they won't be devastating to our lives. We're encouraged by hope by understanding God will help us walk through our valleys.

Sometimes we're called to stand in the gap for those who hurt—by praying and being available to help them. It's amazing how God honors even a small outreach of a cup of cold water or a shoulder to cry on.

Cling tenaciously to the Word of God! It is only as we follow His wisdom that ultimately, we see our situations work out for good. We may not always find purpose and plan in things that happen. I'm thankful that we don't have to understand everything. We may never comprehend this side of heaven, but we pray for the faith and confidence in a loving Father to work things out so they bring something beneficial to us and/or those who watch us. We remind ourselves, "He loves us and cares about what happens in our lives."

Jesus set the example by holding steady in the face of the worst possible storm cloud. He endured the excruciating pain of the cross, and even experienced joy, because He knew the sacrifice of his life offered a redemptive plan for all mankind. Jesus was God's ultimate gift for a world trapped under the dark clouds of sin. As we comprehend the horror of what Jesus went through, then surely our spirits are buoyed to hold steady under any dark cloud that looms overhead.

BIRTHING NEW HOPE

A woman in labor anticipates a beautiful new life as a result of her struggle. "When a woman gives birth, she has a hard time, there's no getting around it. But when the baby is born, there is joy in the birth. This new life in the world wipes out the memory of pain. The sadness you have right now is similar to that pain, but the coming joy is also similar" (Jn. 16:22-24 MSG). When we are in the midst of trouble, we need to understand God may be birthing something beautiful through our pain.

God observes us carefully in rough times, watching for evidence that we're firmly founded on the Rock. Unlike the foolish man who built his house on the sand, we've made the decision to place our faith and trust in Jesus as our rock-solid foundation. When the rains come, the waters will rise, but we're confident— we'll hold steady throughout the storm.

Jesus is the silver lining that encircles every dark cloud that drifts over the horizon. This silver lining might well represent the doorway of hope. There's an old saying: "Into every life some rain must fall." Without rain, plants won't produce a harvest. We become strong and fruitful— not in spite of, but because of the things we encounter. We're grateful we're not so fragile that we must be encased in a problem-free bubble. With no challenges, we'll likely grow complacent and we certainly won't send deep roots into God.

When the children of Israel struggled in the desert for forty years, God sent a cloud to cover them during the day, to shelter them from the blistering heat. Today, we have the shadow of His wings to rest under. He never intended for the heat of our struggles to destroy us. Heat will either harden or soften us. We've been burned by people and experiences, but in the process, we determine the scorching heat of trouble will soften our hearts until they melt in submission—so that God can continue to mold us.

PRAISE GOD FOR RULING OVER THE CLOUDS

Clouds provide protection as well as refreshing rain, so plants produce their crops. The clean, fresh smell of the earth after the rain delights us because we know that crops will soon begin to grow. Our steadfastness in stormy seasons emits a fresh, clean smell that blesses those around us. God produces new growth when we refuse to let dark clouds ruin our lives. When we stand strong during the storms, the fruit of patience and faithfulness grow profusely.

When we're in the midst of our personal storms, our Father encourages us to pray and look past the struggles. We know His creative power is working because He resides above the clouds. It's appropriate for us to look up and remember He reigns above every bad circumstance. Praise His Holy Name!

At the end of the age, when Jesus returns, it may be a dark day—when hopelessness has generated ominous clouds across the heavens. Jesus has promised to break through those clouds with shouts of victory over every evil force.

Indeed, the return of Jesus will come with power beyond description. "The people will see the Son of Man coming in the clouds, with power and great glory" (Mk. 13:26 NCV). This is a wondrous and victorious picture of Jesus ruling and reigning over every principality and power and dark evil of this world.

When that great day comes, we'll not depend on our own resources. Every eye will behold Him and every knee will bow. Everyone will be convinced—He is the Lord of Lords and the King of Kings. Suddenly, the Light of revelation will burst forth and people of every tribe, tongue, and nation will realize that He has been there all along—watching to see us through every circumstance that came our way. The enemy is defeated while we are protected. Praise God, Jesus is coming again!

THINGS TO CONSIDER

1. How can you keep your attitude right when everything seems to be going wrong?

2. List any bad memories that still plague you.

3. What negative emotions come up for you when things don't go as you want them to?

4. Can you control negative emotions?

5. Do you realize how a bad mood can affect others around you?

6. What value is there in tears?

7. What can you do that will make you laugh?

8. Do you ever blame God when things go wrong?

9. How might Satan try to defeat you when you're experiencing trouble?

10. How can you look beyond your troubles?

CHAPTER 6

ALL SHOOK UP

"...when the keepers of the house tremble..." (Eccl. 12:3 NIV).

With the onset of age, it's not uncommon for Parkinson's disease or general weaknesses to cause people's hands to shake or tremble. Handwriting may become less legible. And since doctors already have the reputation of poor handwriting, pity the poor pharmacists who attempt to read an *older* doctor's prescriptions.

Linda* took her five-year-old, Betsy*, to see her Aunt Sue*, who had advanced Parkinson's disease. On the way home Betsy said, "Mom, we need to pray for Aunt Sue."

"That's a great idea. Remind me tonight and we'll do that."

"But we need to pray for her to get saved."

"Honey, Aunt Sue has been a Christian for a long time."

"Then we need to pray she becomes a better Christian."

Linda whirled around to face Betsy, "What in the world are you talking about?"

Eyes wide with childish innocence, Betsy explained, "Well, our memory verse in class yesterday was, 'The righteous will never be shaken'."

This verse is a reminder; we're not to be shaken on the inside, even when we tremble on the outside. Fear is often the underlying cause for people to shake. Though fear is a God-given emotion, it seems to have been originally designed for flight or fight. Since we aren't in the fleeing or fighting mode much these days, this stuffed energy flutters around inside as free-floating anxiety and interferes with clear thinking and performance.

FEARS CAN BE IMMOBILIZING

Even when I became an adult, ominous threats of danger seemed to loom around every dark corner. Quite possibly it began as a child, when I listened to scary radio programs. (Does that date me or what?) One ongoing serial was called *Inner Sanctum Mystery*. Chills ran down my spine when the program began with a door squeaking open and then closing with a heavy thud. My friends and I also told spooky stories and went to horror movies. We pushed the limits by going to the cemetery to tell ghost stories. After a time, fear haunted me everywhere I went.

A limb scratching against the screen at night would catch my attention and scare me spit-less. I was convinced something or someone was crawling into my dark bedroom. My trembling and racing heart was every bit as affected as if some monster were actually about to devour me. Fear, plus imagination, always leads to panic.

I prayed for God to give me the ability to reel in my wild fears. It took years of prayer for me to truly accept that God does take care of His children. I continued to remind myself of Jesus' promise—to leave us a peace that was beyond anything the world ever experienced. This sounded good, but I realized I had the responsibility to slam the door and not allow myself to be exposed to fearful surroundings. I knew if I kept entertaining spooky thoughts, it would chisel a chink in my armor and allow fear to come and wreak havoc with my emotions. To this day, I refuse to watch scary movies or television programs.

In my early years of marriage, a portion of fear turned into another facet—worry. Carey told me when I didn't have enough to worry about; I'd look for someone else with problems—to help them worry. I hated to admit it, but he was right. I'd wring my hands with anxiety, rubbing fearful possibilities between my fingers. When I made an attempt to offer my anxiety up to God, He seemed to whisper, "If you'll get your grubby little hands off, I'll take care of things."

Carey traveled, and sometimes he'd be late coming home. A few times, my irrational fears escalated until I called the highway department to see if any wrecks had been reported on his route. One dreary night as I paced the floor, I planned his funeral and decided what I'd wear on that fateful day! Obviously, I needed to repent for my lack of faith. I prayed I'd overcome paralyzing anxiety and worrisome fears. In time, He lowered my anxiety level until it fell within normal limits. "Thank you, Lord."

Inordinate anxiety is the springboard to worry and fear. It is accompanied with a passel of apprehensions, distresses and dread. Satan edges in with tidbits of these *hors d'oeuvres,* and every chance he gets; he serves us a whole platter of fear.

Fear is not only dangerous—it is also contagious. When people around us observe and pick up on our fears, it can easily escalate to mob reaction. The Word teaches us we can come against the instigator of this turmoil by humbly coming before God to enlist His power to resist the devil. It is only His authority that forces the enemy to back off.

When the planes crashed into the Twin Towers, Linda called her husband repeatedly at work to inform him of the latest details. She stayed glued to the TV, watching the replays of the collapsing buildings. Anxiety escalated. Finally, her husband said, "Linda, do us both a favor and turn off the TV. Find something to distract you so you're not consumed by this tragedy."

§

Everyone is aware of how much worry drains us physically. Most of us would rather scrub floors or dig ditches than to be locked in a cage with worry eroding our peace. Instead, we can choose to huddle closer to God. "God is a safe place to hide, ready to help when we need Him. We stand fearless at the cliff-edge of doom, courageous in sea storm and earthquake, before the rush and roar of oceans, the tremors that shift mountains" (Ps. 46:2-3 MSG). He alone can infuse us with enough courage to stop trembling.

Worry does nothing to help solve the problem—it compounds it. It damages our health and interferes with clear thinking. In a short period of time, I lost five family members through death. Each time the phone jangled I jumped, because I was afraid something had happened to another loved one. When we nurture seeds of worrisome thinking, we water them with a list of *what-ifs*. That causes them to sprout and affect every aspect of our lives.

§

God often builds our emotional immune system by inoculating us with small doses of challenges. Even simple things like traffic, waiting for a doctor's report, or looking for lost keys can send people into a tail spin. When we learn to deal with small things, often the bigger problems become manageable. We take as our motto an old saying, "Yard by yard, life is hard, but inch by inch, life's a cinch." Our goal is to come to the point where we can exclaim, "When besieged, I'm calm as a baby. When all hell breaks loose, I'm collected and cool" (Ps. 27:3 MSG)."

§

When I had Kathy, my first child, I decided to use the then little known method of *Natural Childbirth*. I'd read some articles and a 'how-to' book on relaxing, exercise and proper breathing. With my doctor's consent, I followed each step as labor progressed. I concentrated on staying calm. In the labor room I remembered to take one contraction at a time—breathing, relaxing and watching the clock, declaring each minute accomplished its purpose of bringing me closer to delivery. Nurses couldn't understand my composure. However, I didn't have to wonder why they called it labor; it *was* hard work. This taught me to live in the peace and the power of the present moment. This discipline prepared me for other struggles in life—to handle situations one step at a time.

THERE ARE VALID CONCERNS

Carey had gone to the hospital for tests. Rectal bleeding had been a concern. He called me on the phone. His fearful words were barely audible. "It's cancer."

I gasped. "I'll be right there." I cradled the phone slowly on its base as shock and sorrow rose from within—until they reached my eyes and spilled over in the form of tears. I called a friend, who rushed over and offered a shoulder to cry on. She shook me gently. "Cry your eyes out on the way to the hospital, but pull yourself together before going into his room."

I followed her advice and paused momentarily outside Carey's door, to take a deep breath and utter a quick prayer. Going near his bedside, I faked confidence, "Hey Tiger, it looks like we have a battle on our hands. You know, we're in this fight together." Day after day, we determined to face the future by dealing only with the battle of the day.

Science has proven that worry and anxiety lower the immune system, as well as damage us emotionally and spiritually. After Carey's diagnosis, I periodically fought headaches and stomach aches, to the point of being nauseated at times.

Tension caused me to make mistakes on my job. Fear revved the engines of my nervous system until I became exhausted. Like a sponge, it sopped up my energy and wrung me out, leaving me limp and confused. Carey's well-being involved fighting for his life. My battles were emotional. I fought against fearful attacks that stemmed from bad news. Day by day, God taught me to sit down and untangle the knots of yesterday's problems that threatened to keep me tied to fear.

I refused to get bound up with tomorrow's dark threats. Friends offered appropriate Scripture that helped me deal with each day's struggle. Tunnel vision became a friend by helping me concentrate on the one thing facing us at the moment. Like the old fashioned blinders on a horse, it kept me focused on what lay directly ahead. The Lord's faithfulness held me steady as Carey's health deteriorated.

In facing the challenge, Carey and I attempted to live in day tight compartments—closing the doors behind us to protect us from yesterday's battles. We kept future doors locked, knowing threats of pain and death mocked us on the other side. I made a commitment to Carey that whatever time we had together, we'd make the best of it. I made a conscious effort to do things that pleased him. It made me wonder, "Why did I wait for disaster before searching for special things to please him?"

We can choose to run to God immediately when worry plagues us. We remind ourselves that He alone is capable of handling any situation that comes up life. He can infuse us with the courage to hold on to Him as He controls the shaking.

THE FUTURE IS IN GOD'S HAND

Most of us have concerns about growing older. When I lost my retirement money through a bad investment, I was afraid my money would expire before I did. Diseases and disabilities showing up in my peers increased my own concerns. When I lost things or forgot something, I'd wonder if I were experiencing the onset of Alzheimer's.

Fear is distracting. We lose things and can't remember where we put them—though the item may be right in front of our faces. Decision-making becomes more difficult. Rational thinking eludes us. When one dwells on aging problems excessively, uneasiness flits about as another form of fear.

It's saddening and disconcerting to lose older friends and loved ones in death. The problem is evident when I go to a family or high school reunion and take note of shrinking numbers. We're forced to face our own mortality.

If we're not careful, we can open a Pandora's Box of imaginary demons of 'what-ifs' that can immobilize our thoughts and actions. We must depend on God to show us how to slam the lid shut and trust in Him. "I saw God before me for all time. Nothing can shake me; he's right by my side. I'm glad from the inside out, ecstatic; I've pitched my tent in the land of hope." (Acts 2:28 MSG). Hold steady, friend. God walks beside us. In Him we find our blessed hope.

Reasonable concern over any situation is healthy and God intended for us to use common sense for our protection. A police officer spoke at a meeting I attended and told us to never ignore gut-level feelings of caution. He said, "Many who ignore such warnings suffer dire consequences."

Especially as we grow older, it is essential for us to listen to God, rather than react to others with undependable emotions.

Emotions can act as a hook, snagging us in the jaw and dragging us around. We build confidence in the One who is the epitome of strength and peace. He has invited us to enter into His rest with Him. We need to remind ourselves that we can hold steady in life because He works powerfully in us.

God gives us opportunities—not only to accept the challenges of this stage of life—but He has equipped us with the ability to adjust. When I find myself feeling shaky, I search for appropriate Scripture for assurance that God is with me. Psalms 91 helps me hunker down and stand strong when fear assaults.

BENEFITS OF A CALM SPIRIT

We find that when we're not all shaken by circumstances, we're able to think more creatively. Fresh ideas often pop into my mind when I'm falling asleep, during the night or early in the morning—when I'm in a peaceful and quiet atmosphere. New and creative ideas flicker across my brain, like clicking the remote to a different TV channel. Calm composure is essential to creative thinking.

I've heard of some who wake up in the night with a new song lilting across their consciousness. An acquaintance dreamed of a unique invention, for which he later got a patent. Some keep a flashlight and notepad by their bed, to write down new ideas that drift through their minds during the night. Perhaps that's the reason we should sleep on a decision before acting on it. Rest has a way of ushering us into the presence of a creative God. His voice is never clearer than when our minds are at peace. As we learn to be still, we get to know Him better.

Jesus set us an example by committing His spirit into the hands of His Father. We have the same privilege to release our fears into the hand of the One who rules the universe. "And I gave them eternal life, so they will never be lost. No one can snatch them out of my hand" (Jn. 10:28 CEV). How reassuring to know God holds us in the palm of His hand, where all the forces of hell cannot pry us loose.

Philippians contains the powerful prerequisite to peace. "Do not be anxious about anything, but in everything, by prayer and petition, with thanksgiving, present your requests to God. And the peace of God that transcends all understanding will guard your hearts and your minds in Christ Jesus" (Phil. 4:6-7 NIV). We seal a package of prayer with grateful thanksgiving because He holds the solution for every problem.

Have you ever noticed how much easier it is to remain at peace in the midst of praise and worship? I know of groups in a foreign country that worship in house churches—where their services are sometimes broken into by the police. Once, the authorities came bursting into their worship service and started breaking things and hitting the members. The Christians began to sing louder. This so frustrated the assailants, they stormed out of the meeting place. Can you imagine the confusion the militia felt when the Christians remained unflappable?

It's wonderful that God is not only aware of the mounds of worrisome dirt in our lives, but is also concerned with the dust particles of anxieties and apprehensions that are sprinkled across our existence.

We Christians live in an ongoing spiritual battle against the devil. Our battles are often fierce, as the enemy comes to shake us up. Sometimes we're hit by a barrage of problems. Satan is not beneath sending his envoys in waves of consecutive attacks. It is amazing how calm we can remain if we predetermine that God is our defense.

There is an acronym of: **F**ear is **E**vidence that **A**ppears **R**eal. Fear is stirred up by imagining potential dangers. President Roosevelt, in his fireside chats during World War II, reminded his listeners, "The only thing to fear, is fear itself."

Our minds cannot focus in two different directions at the same time. We lose our fears by focusing on God's boldness and strength, rather than our own resources. As the Wisdom and Power of the universe, He offers to undergird us with His righteous right hand. It makes me feel safer to realize He holds me in the palm of His hand. The older we get, the more we need that kind of assurance. "Ah, thanks, that's much better."

It's time to pitch our tents in the land of hope. The God of love rules over this land where we plan to take up permanent residence. His love forces fear out. Our heavenly Father provides our homeland security. We pledge our allegiance to stand under the King's authority and protection. Fear doesn't hold office in His house of representatives, nor can it wield any power in His regime.

He is our Jehovah Nissi, our banner. His banner of love flies high above us in a land where we can be confident and composed. This flag is never lowered to half mast, signifying death or defeat. This banner needs to be raised, rather than lowered during the storms of life.

THINGS TO CONSIDER

1. How can a Christian hold steady during difficult times?

2. Can you admit an area of emotional weakness in your life?

3. What can you do to graciously accept physical weakness as a part of aging?

4. Do you have other fears related to aging?

5. Do you spend too much time worrying about what is happening, or may happen, in your later years?

6. Do you have difficulty going to sleep at night because you are anxious?

7. How can you learn to take your thoughts captive?

8. Are you learning to trust that God can bring good things from bad circumstances?

9. Do you ever take time to sit and think creatively—to write a poem, to play or sing a song or think about what heaven will be like?

10. Can you think of creative ways to reach out to others?

CHAPTER 7

WEAK BONES AND HEAVY LOADS

"…the strong men stoop…" (Eccl. 12:3 NIV).

Osteoporosis often causes older people to stoop. It advances as subtly and as cautiously as a mouse nibbling away at cheese in a trap. We often notice it in others before we are aware of our own shoulders hunching. My doctor told me I had the beginnings of osteoporosis and recommended I take some medication. I suppose I will. Refusing to take the meds might indicate I'm stupid—and as a result, I'd end up stooped.

§

My brother, Don, was never tall. As he grew older and bone density lessened, he lost precious inches. When a friend teased him about his short stature, his wife, Mickey, stood by and spoke proudly, "He's about the biggest man I know." Don's integrity and strength of character quickly explained why she felt he stood head and shoulders above most men. Regardless of our physical height or how insignificant we may feel, we too, may stand tall in the sight of God.

OTHER REASONS FOR STOOPING

Some older people may stoop from trudging around as if they're carrying the weight of the world on their shoulders. This becomes evident—emotionally and physically. Not unlike termites working to destroy the structure of a house, discouragement chomps away at our support structure—our feelings of significance and self-confidence—until our spirit crumbles and we're left pathetically bent over. God, as the great exterminator, is concerned and competent to destroy these destructive forces. Jesus spoke to those of us who carry weight that is too heavy. "Come to me, all of you who are tired and have heavy loads, and I will give you rest... I am gentle and humble in spirit, and you will find rest for your lives. The burden that I ask you to accept is easy; the load I give you to carry is light" (Matt. 11:28 NCV).

It takes more effort to cling to optimism when we are overloaded with the cares of the world. However, rather than whine and complain, we look for assistance. God tells us He sent His Son to help in troubling times. Jesus headed out on His mission empowered by the Holy Spirit. He healed those beaten down by the devil. Satan, the liar, tells us we're growing weak and pokes fun at our bodies. He reminds us that we can't handle life as we once did. His accusations are partially true. But we remind him that we're equipped for everything God commissions us to do, in each stage of life.

In later years, God presents us with the challenge to rely more completely on Him. When we can no longer depend on our own strength or leverage to lift heavy loads, Jesus is available as the One with unlimited power. He encourages us to cast our cares on Him. (I must admit, I told Him, "I think I needed casting lessons.")

To be a good witness for God, we'll not go around with our emotions and our bodies all bent out of shape. To the contrary, we stand proud by proclaiming all God has done for us throughout our lives. With the Lord's strength coursing through our veins, we straighten up in God's bright presence to celebrate and worship our Messiah, Jesus, in all His majesty and power.

Age may well be our crucible, testing how steadfast we'll stand as the ravages of time pummel our bodies. They no longer look, feel, or function as they did when we were young. Be confident, we can hold to God's promises by being spiritually anchored, even when everything about our bodies cries out in weakness.

Centuries ago older people went to sit around the market place, to share with those who passed by. "This is what the Lord Almighty says: Once again men and women of ripe old age will sit in the streets of Jerusalem, each with cane in hand because of his age" (Zech. 8:4 NIV). They sat there to *give out* rather than looking for *a hand out*.

USING GOD TO LEAN ON

Some accuse believers of using Christianity as a crutch. I certainly do! I lean heavily on that staff, with no apologies. Not only would I stoop, but without Him holding me up, I'd fall flat on my face. I'm thankful His strength is available to me.

How good it is to know that when we wander off the narrow way, God comes looking for us. Jesus is pictured as the Shepherd searching for lost sheep—for those of us who have strayed. He binds up our wounds and carries us when we are weary. When I feel tired and bent over, I like to think of Jesus picking me up and hoisting me on His shoulders.

WE WERE MEANT TO CARRY A LOAD

This is not a time for us to opt out and become free-loaders. Nor is it time for us to collapse into an easy chair, expecting everyone to wait on us. Complacency isn't a godly characteristic. Our Creator designed us to carry our share, for as long as we're here. The stronger carry heavier loads, while the rest of us carry less. We're not to show up at a pity party with demands: "I've taken care of everyone else—it's time now for everyone else to look after me."

Periodically, it's good to assess what we're assigned to carry. When our strength and energy begin to wane, we may need to let go of some responsibilities. It's always important to evaluate where our current responsibility should end, and the responsibility of others should kick in. God's wisdom helps us make appropriate adjustments. The Lord has designed a good balance for us throughout our life.

HANDICAPS FROM BIRTH OR INJURIES

Nick Vujicic, from Australia, came into this world without arms or legs. There was no medical explanation. He travels worldwide, offering his message of hope and encouragement. He has a powerful DVD called *Life Without Limbs—From No Limbs to No Limits*. In this video, he explains how he refused to allow his handicap to immobilize him.

He fought with depression in early years, and would have dared to take his life. However, he laughs, "Without arms or legs, how in the world could I do myself in?" His parents, faced with Nick' incredible disability, struggled to keep their faith from wavering. When they fully accepted there was no way to correct his problem, they resolved to devise ways for him to become as independent as possible.

Nick has a little flipper off his hip; a couple of appendages protrude from it. With those, he can type forty words a minute. With great tenacity, faith and a sense of humor, he accomplishes unimaginable tasks.

Now, he thanks God for his body. Because of his unusual disability, thousands come to hear him tell his story and proclaim the Good News of Jesus. God opens doors for him in countries and places inaccessible to other Christians. When he speaks of his overcoming victory, people listen with rapt attention and are in awe of his peace and joy, because he not only accepts his body, but he has found the answer to what God can do through his great handicap. He gives the glory to God. His shoulders don't slump—and he refuses to allow his spirit to stoop.

The strongest man in the world appears weak beside Nick, who has overcome incomprehensible problems with God-given strength. "My grace is enough; it's all you need. My strength comes into its own in your weakness . . . Now I take limitations in stride, and with good cheer, these limitations that cut me down to size—abuse, accidents, opposition, bad breaks. I just let Christ take over! And so the weaker I get, the stronger I become" (2 Cor. 12:10 MSG). It's not always clear how the power of Christ can overshadow difficult situations. However, our Gracious Father often teaches us step by step—how He can take what Satan meant for evil and use it for good.

There are those who've become handicapped as the result of accidents. Joni Erickson Tada became a quadriplegic. As a beautiful teenager, she dove into water, hit bottom and broke her neck. She has touched the lives of people around the world, even though she is unable to use her limbs. She explains how, through dogged determination and her faith in God, she overcame many of her limitations. She's an author and on television as a talented vocalist and motivational speaker. She developed remarkable artistic talent by drawing with a paint brush clenched between her teeth. The excuses I use for not overcoming a few stumbling blocks of aging are pathetic in the light of these two outstanding Christians.

§

Imagine an older athlete who enters the locker room for the last time to hang up his jersey. Previously, he's received his self-worth from cheering crowds. As he stands there now, he may have drooping shoulders, choking back tears. He realizes other athletes have stood where he now stands, but that gives him little comfort. He is devastated when he realizes that he will no longer be the star of the game.

Suppose he learns to take pride in standing before God rather than multitudes of fans? By faith, he can hear the Lord standing and shouting His approval, cheering him on. Then, this athlete could accept God's offer to be drafted to enter another race, where he'll never be disqualified because of age, disability or lack of strength. He'll no longer sit on the sidelines, wishing he could be out on the playing field. He can respond to God—calling for him to play in the championship game of life.

A wise, retiring athlete refuses to remain stuck, staring at his past accolades. His reward comes as he realizes it's not a gold medal he's after, but a golden crown and a welcome mat that is laid out on streets of gold. "You've all been to the stadium and seen the athlete's race. Everyone runs; one wins. Run to win. All good athletes train hard. They do it for a gold medal that tarnishes and fades. You're after one that's gold eternally" (1 Cor. 9:24 MSG). In the Christian race, God plans for all of us to be winners.

How Do We Look to Our Later Days?

We look to the future—as either a dream or a dread. We're wise if we live today as if it were a gift, which it is. That's why they call it the present! We have the opportunity to wrap the gift of today in peace and joy and to offer it to everyone around us. Not only will this help others stand tall, but we find ourselves standing straight. As we encourage others, we are encouraged.

A bad attitude is worse than any physically debilitating handicap. Sour attitudes are exhibited by far too many people when they face the impositions of aging. I admit, it is disturbing to discover Father Time hacking away at health and energy, but we have a choice as to how we respond.

When we lived in Idaho years ago an older church member constantly complained about his health—his arthritis, a headache, a belly ache and his lack of energy. He added to the list—

his poor finances, bad crops and complaints about his children. The more he talked, the more his shoulders drooped. Carey listened to him until he'd had enough. One Sunday, after listening to his laundry list of gripes, Carey looked him in the eye. "Brother Grumbly," (Ha. Not his real name.) "I'm going to keep asking you how you feel until one day you'll tell me you're feeling good."

He shook his head and replied, "I never will." He'd made the decision to never change. It's sad when one not only discourages himself but is a discouragement to everyone within hearing distance. The more we review our problems, the worse we feel.

Those who are bowed down with problems miss seeing opportunities to reach out to others. My sister attends church with a woman who is actually bent double. She has difficulty getting around, even with a walker. However, as she twists her head to look up, she radiantly smiles and speaks to everyone she meets. Her body, not her spirit, is stooped over.

§

As a teen, I was a fair athlete and would do most anything on a dare. Now that I'm older, I admit my limitations and back away from tasks God has not assigned to me. "I have strength for all things in Christ who empowers me. I am ready for anything and equal to anything through Him who infuses inner strength into me; I am self-sufficient in Christ's sufficiency" (Phil. 2:13 AMP).

God isn't that interested in our jumping high hurdles or knocking a ball out of the park, but He expects us to incorporate His strength to do what needs to be done. This may well be the last inning of the game, but when He pitches us the ball, He intends for us to at least swing at it. We depend on Him to be our coach until we the game is over.

As a person grows older, there's not only the tendency to stoop, but a danger of falling. It is most important that we don't fall away from Him. "And now to him who can keep you on your feet, standing tall in his bright presence, fresh and celebrating— to our one God, our only Savior, through Jesus Christ our Master, be glory, majesty and strength and rule before all time and now, and to the end of time. Yes" (Jude 24-25 MSG).

Even during our latter years, we can choose to be a blessing, not a burden. If we were ever to become totally helpless and have to be cared for, we'll never be an unbearable burden as long as we refuse to grumble, complain or gripe. Though flat on our backs, we still have the option of remaining pleasant, peaceful and prayerful, rather than pitiful, pathetic and pessimistic.

Physical strength will fail after a time, but spiritual and emotional strength can grow stronger every day. In the meantime— and it can be a *mean time*, we can lift others up rather than weigh them down.

THINGS TO CONSIDER

1. How do you think one can stand tall spiritually?

2. What does it mean to cast your cares on the Lord?

3. Have you ever viewed aging as a test?

4. Have you shouldered a load that should be the responsibility of someone else?

5. Can you think of someone who has an incredible attitude in spite of great handicaps?

6. Do others inspire you or discourage you as you watch them deal with difficult situations?

7. Do you tend to be more optimistic or pessimistic with your thoughts and words?

8. Are you choosing to be a blessing or a burden at this point in life?

9. Are there times when you want to give up?

10. Why are your later years a greater opportunity to depend more on the Lord?

CHAPTER **8**

EATING PROBLEMS AND OTHER FRUSTRATIONS

"...the grinders cease because they are few..." (Eccl. 12:3 NIV).

TOOTH OR CONSEQUENCES?

No doubt Solomon referred to the golden-agers who lose their teeth. Gums can't grind food. Years ago in the States, and even now in third world countries, it's not uncommon for people to begin to lose some or all of their teeth as they grow older. I felt bad when Dad lost his teeth because of a gum disease. All I could say was, "Well, Dad. . .gum it!"

Dentists have looked in my mouth and said, "It looks like you've spent a lot of time in a dentist's chair." They're right, and on some of those visits, I've had experiences I'd prefer to forget. One dentist told me he might break my jaw trying to extract wisdom teeth that were impacted. He didn't break my jaw, but my hair stood on end when he said, "Don't worry, I invented a special tool for this kind of job. I call it my crow bar!" Another dentist broke a drill bit at the bottom of my tooth while doing a root canal job. However, I'm still grateful there are measures to help me keep my grinders.

When I taught in a prison, a prisoner asked, "Would you open your mouth?"

"Why?"

"You've got a lot of gold in there."

I closed my mouth quickly, not daring to think what he wanted to do: "Oh, not much," I mumbled and immediately changed the subject.

I once fell and knocked my bottom teeth back and pushed the upper teeth into my gums. The orthodontist repositioned my teeth and wired them together. I assumed I'd lose weight, but found I could suck more calories through a straw than most people can shovel in with a spoon. Grinding ceased for a while, but the food chain only dropped to the simpler level. The only thing I could chew on without discomfort was decisions.

§

God commissioned us to feed the hungry. Grinding ceases for some, not because of lack of teeth, but because they have nothing to chew on. When we lived in Denver, we received a call asking if we could pick up four children who'd been abandoned by their mother. The children ranged from two weeks to five years of age.

We arrived at the concrete block shell of a home and went in. The smell of filth and burned oatmeal caused us to gag. We placed our hands over our noses and mouths. The gaunt father stood at the door with his head hanging. "I can't take care of them anymore. That burnt oatmeal on the stove is all we've had to eat the past three days."

We gathered the children and put them in the car. The two older ones pressed their little noses to the car window and waved to their daddy until he was out of sight. We drove home in silence. There, I discovered the baby's diaper hadn't been changed for so long it had to be soaked off with warm water. I watched in horror as blood oozed to the surface of her tender bottom. The tiny child whimpered, too weak to cry. She could take no more than one or two ounces of milk until her stomach stretched to normal size.

When I opened a jar of junior baby food for the fourteen month old, the five year old snatched the lid and licked it. I began to peel carrots for supper and she grabbed the peelings off the counter and stuffed them in her mouth. My heart ached—I'd never been around starving children before.

We kept them a few weeks, along with our own—aged three, two and six months, until arrangements were made for their adoption. Their mother signed papers, giving them up. She never returned to say good-bye.

When leaving for their new homes, their little faces were shining and their hair—squeaky clean. They were vibrant and happy. They'd never be abandoned again. Never again would they feel hunger pains.

FEED THE SPIRITUALLY HUNGRY

But even more pathetic than the plight of these children are the multitudes of spiritually malnourished—even among the rich.

There are many who have a craving, a hunger inside, longing for something more. God longs to fill that emptiness with Himself—to fill us and top us off with the whipped cream of encouragement and a cherry of deep satisfaction.

Jesus was born in a village called Bethlehem, which means 'house of bread.' There, He was placed in a feed trough, in a stable. In His adult ministry He proclaimed, "I am the bread that gives life! No one who comes to me will ever be hungry. No one who has faith in me will ever be thirsty" (Jn. 6:35 CEV).

After Jesus had fasted for forty days in the wilderness, the devil tempted Him by reminding Him—He could turn the stones to bread. Jesus didn't hesitate. He told him straight out, "It is written, man does not live on bread alone" (Luke 4:4 NIV). The Father sent Jesus to satisfy our spiritual hunger. If we fail to be filled, it is only because we refuse to come to the table.

§

The Holy Spirit gave me a wake-up call when I realized how I continued to stress and strain because I wanted to be significant. I was independent—gritting my teeth and attempting to conquer every challenge I faced. If anyone ever said, "I double dog dare you," I'd break my neck to prove I could take a dare and do almost anything. When I humbled myself and asked Jesus to lead my life, God adopted me and invited me to His table, to eat of the Bread of Life along with His family. Jesus reminded us that God sent manna to the children of Israel in the desert. He explained He is the one who gives us true bread from heaven. As we develop our taste for heavenly bread, Jesus becomes our provision to satisfy our appetites— forever.

I love to eat. I eat to celebrate, I eat when I'm depressed, I eat to be sociable and I eat when I'm bored. *Bon appetit.* I hope the Scripture that reads "their God is their belly" wasn't written for my sake. I have to admit, there's a temptation to stuff my stomach and placate my conscience with the resolution to "eat, drink and be merry, for tomorrow I diet."

Some are picky eaters. I have little patience with those who only eat meat and potatoes or refuse to eat leftovers. Jesus reminded us, "Don't fuss about what's on the table at mealtimes or if the clothes in your closet are in fashion. There is far more to your inner life than the food you put in your stomach, more to your outer appearance than the clothes you hang on your body" (Matt. 6:25 MSG). The shelves in most of our pantries and refrigerators are well stocked with multiple choices of food. Often I stand in front of the refrigerator with the door open. I'm not especially hungry, but looking to see if anything there appeals to my taste buds.

LOOK FOR WHAT OTHERS NEED

Instead of looking for what I want, perhaps it's time to find what others need. I could go for a period of time without buying groceries and probably live the rest of my life without buying new clothing. As we look around during this time of financial crisis, we discover more people who need basic nourishment to satisfy their hunger.

Christians should be known as people who feed the hungry, give water to the thirsty and find homes for the homeless. They'll be there to clothe those shivering from the cold. They'll visit the shut-ins and those in prison. I pray we'll always be more interested in reaching out to others in need than wondering what we're going to wear to social gatherings or where we're going to go out to eat.

Our affluent society seldom realizes how we've allowed material possessions to become the focal point of our lives. God is calling people from all walks of life to come to His banquet table to be filled with a spiritual feast. I had a Christian woman from a foreign nation visit in my home. As she sat down to eat, she marveled, "It must be so hard to be a Christian here. You have so many things to distract you."

§

Eddie Grindley came from Ireland as a young boy. He ended up in Los Angeles, where he worked in a hotel as a bell hop. He lived a sordid life —drinking, gambling and rough living.

A pretty young lady, Stella, worked at the same hotel. He kept asking her to go out with him. She refused his offer until he agreed to go with her to worship. Since she'd given him no other option, he reluctantly went to church.

Eddie fell in love with Stella and with the Lord. His conversion so impacted him that he went out to the streets and slums to bring in those he identified with—the winos and the indigent, smelly and hungry. He marched them down the aisle of the church to seat them on front pews. Some members were repulsed and indignant. They tried to discourage Eddie—or at least have him seat these derelicts on back rows—but he remained undaunted.

Eddie was exuberant when many of the street people responded to Christ, because they found He satisfied their spiritual hunger. He watched as the Word of God transformed many of them—until they became healthy and strong in the Lord. Some moved back into society and found jobs. Happily, they responded to a spiritual hand-up. For those who only came for a hand-out, Eddie continued to feed and clothe them.

Jesus told of the socially acceptable being invited to a banquet. When the occasion came, they weaseled out. He was angry and sent for those out on the highways and byways to come enjoy his banquet. The King of Kings goes to great lengths to prepare for His guests. When people blow Him off, He's outraged and extends His invitation to bring in anyone who is in need of a square meal. He surprises the misfits and the homeless by offering to give them the feast of their lives.

Some toss the Lord's invitation like trash, along with junk mail. "That's what I mean when I say, 'Many get invited; only a few make it'" (Matt. 22:14 MSG). Let's never throw God's invitation aside. We look forward to being at His table. We'll be more than content for Him to seat us wherever He chooses.

COMMUNION

When eating the Last Supper, Jesus took the bread, offered thanks and gave it to his disciples saying, "Take it; this is my body." Then He took the cup, gave thanks and offered it to them and they all drank from it. "This is my blood of the covenant, which is poured out for many" (Mark 14:22-24 NIV). Communion gives us the opportunity for Jesus to become more and more a part of us. This is a time for us to bond with Jesus, as well as with fellow believers. There's a Hebrew expression, *'l'chaim*—to life!' We make this our toast as we eat the bread and drink the fruit of the vine. It is a life-giving experience.

A HUNGER FOR GOD

I prayed for a fresh infilling of the Holy Spirit and found myself devouring Scripture, chewing on the meat of deeper meanings. I picked up the Bible—not just out of habit, but with a yearning to know more about the Author. Reading the Bible is no longer a matter of checking off another thing on my to-do list, but it moves to top priority on my 'needs' list. I discovered by reading God's Word that He has an individual purpose for each one of us. As we develop a taste for God, we grow healthy and strong in the Lord.

There's no need for us to be content with crumbs— the bits and pieces of God's Word we pick up while attending church. Jesus has already told us to live by every word that comes from the mouth of God. This reminds me to stop picking and choosing those things that fit my fancy. The things I've underlined in my Bible are not the only important issues.

As we study more of God's Word, we see Him at work all around us. Deep satisfaction doesn't come from a quick snack, but from eating a full meal. "You're blessed when you've worked up a good appetite for God. He's food and drink in the best meal you'll ever eat" (Matt. 5:6 MSG). We'll be more than just physically filled when we hunger and thirst for righteousness.

Our digestive system is designed to rid our bodies of waste— things that would be counter-productive to good health. Spiritually, we also need to rid our lives of those things that work against our spiritual health—things like malice, pretense, envy and hurtful talk.

We all need God-type nourishment. His special food is a type of antioxidant that wards off every spiritual virus. It builds our immune system against anger, resentment and unforgiveness. His Word helps us grow healthy inside and out.

What a joy to know we can take our every day, ordinary life of eating, sleeping and working to please God. "We may not be much Lord, but I hear you sometimes delight in picking the unlikely. We have nothing else to give. If you have something in mind for us, have at it! Since you adopted us as your children, we're ready to accept whatever you put in front of us on the table. Keep us from turning up our noses at anything on our plates."

Jesus claimed He was nourished by doing God's will. He purposed to finish the work God laid out for Him to do. If we sign up, we won't simply read about how to live—we'll walk it out in the way we think, talk and act.

PREPARING FOR THE LAST JOURNEY

It may not be time for us to pack our bags yet, but travel brochures advertising the life ahead sound exciting. It's God's choice of timing. "Compared to what's coming, living conditions around here seem like a stopover in an unfurnished shack and we're tired of it! We've been given a glimpse of the real thing, our true home in our resurrection bodies! The Spirit of God whets our appetite by giving us a taste of what's ahead. He puts a little of heaven in our hearts so that we'll never settle for less" (2 Cor. 5:5 MSG). The Bread of Life keeps us well-nourished and fit to go.

I watched a reporter interview a street person on TV, a woman who lived under a bridge. She smiled a toothless grin and said, "Let me show you my house of praise." She led the reporter under a bridge and showed him a cardboard structure she'd built to sleep in. Her 'grinders' were few, but obviously the woman satisfied her spiritual hunger by glorifying God.

Our mouths may water as we anticipate the feast God is preparing for us. He's given us some appetizers that help us realize we can "taste and see that He is good." I know He'll prepare the greatest banquet we've ever attended. I anticipate the great Thanksgiving dinner to be served to us when we arrive at home, not just for the holidays, but forever and ever.

THINGS TO CONSIDER

1. Are you helping feed the hungry?

2. Do you encourage and teach those who are spiritually hungry?

3. Are you guilty of picking and choosing what you want to believe in Scripture?

4. Do you find it helpful to read the same scriptures over and over for encouragement?

5. Do your actions prove that physical food is more important to you than spiritual food?

6. Is there a void in your life that needs to be filled?

7. What kind of spiritual food are you getting?

8. Are you satisfied with where you are and what you are doing at this point in life?

9. Do you ask the Holy Spirit to help you know what to pray for?

10. Do you spend time meditating on the Word of God?

CHAPTER 9

I FORGOT WHAT TO REMEMBER

"…and those looking out of the windows grow dim…
" (Eccl. 12:3 NIV).

Our minds begin to lose files and often current events aren't even put in a folder. We once accessed information with efficiency, but now yesterday's events are often irretrievable. What good can come from being a person with Alzheimer's or a caregiver for an individual with this disease? The condition feels like an attack by the enemy to rob, kill and destroy.

A REMARKABLE MYSTERY

Both Jan's father and mother had dementia and were in a nursing home. One day they heard someone in an adjoining room talking and crying. Her father asked a nurse to go get them and bring them into his room. The nurse returned with yet another nurse whose was biting her lip. Her eyes were tear-stained and red.

Jan's father asked what was wrong and the nurse explained she'd just gotten a report from the doctor showing she had a large cancerous tumor. Doctors were urging her to have surgery immediately. Jan's father and mother asked her to come near so they could pray for her. After a fervent prayer for healing, the nurse thanked them and left. She assured them she would let them know about the surgery.

In the operating room, the doctors were amazed when they found no trace of the tumor and no sign of cancer. God's healing touch had worked through those parents whose minds were no longer alert.

Much later the nurse confided, "Jan, I don't think I would be here today if your parents hadn't prayed for me." Her parents couldn't remember praying for the nurse but Jan was thankful that God's Holy Spirit continued to use her parents— even when their minds were slipping away. The older couple continued to encourage both staff and patients.

SOME REMAIN SWEET

Thankfully, some with dementia remain gracious and sweet. Aunt Mary had been through many hardships in her life. In spite of this, I remember Aunt Mary consistently singing and laughing. As the disease eroded her mind, I drove her home from visiting her daughter. The late evening sun began to set, blazing in glorious colors. Aunt Mary pointed and exclaimed, "Isn't that a beautiful . . . picnic?" She chuckled softly, "I can't find my words anymore."

While we still have the ability to think and remember—it's wise to fill the storehouse of our minds with those things that are pure, holy, loving and joyful. Hopefully, we can maintain and retrieve those basic attitudes, even if our brains are not functioning efficiently.

One mother had never been expressive of love or encouragement to others until after she was diagnosed with Alzheimer's. When her daughter visited one day, her mother said, "Honey, you're so beautiful—and you have beautiful teeth, but you have them in upside down." Some of her statements, like this one, were funny, but they were kind. Is it possible that attitudes buried deep inside float to the surface when we can no longer control our thoughts?

Some patients remember old hymns they sang long ago and yet can't remember what happened moments before. It is meaningful for us to sing to them—the old songs as well as contemporary ones. We have the opportunity to fill their rooms with praise and hopefully it will lift their spirits.

Judith sat with her dying mother who was in advanced stages of Alzheimer's. She hovered close to her bedside, holding her hand, praying for her, asking for the Lord's will to be done. Judith fell asleep and dreamed a spiraling cloud rose over her mom's bed. Her mother was in the midst of the cloud— radiant, youthful and beautiful—just as she'd looked when she modeled as a young lady. Judith was startled at the likeness to pictures she'd seen in a magazine that featured her mom.

When Judith woke up, she leaned close and said, "Mom, you can go now. I will be all right and I'll take care of my brothers." She left the nursing home and drove home. When she arrived, she had a message on her answering machine, "Your mother passed away soon after you left." Judith held on to the image of her mother being restored, alive, beautiful and fluent again. "But let me reveal to you a wonderful secret. We will not all die, but we will all be transformed! It will happen in a moment, in the blink of an eye, when the last trumpet is blown. For when the trumpet sounds, those who have died will be raised forever" (1 Cor.15:51-52 NLT).

AGE IS NOT ENTIRELY TO BLAME

Forgetfulness can't always be blamed on aging. For years I've had a problem forgetting where I put car keys, papers and mail. Many times my children stood waiting by the door, ready to leave. One of them would sigh, "We can't go yet—Mom can't find the car keys."

One Sunday the bench where I sat in church jiggled because my muffled laughter shook me inside and out. The preacher had quoted Jesus telling Peter, "And I will give unto you the keys of the Kingdom" (Matt. 16:19 NIV). I bit my lip. *Lord, I'm so glad you didn't give those keys to me, I'd lose them for sure.* I could envision the blast of the trumpet on the last day and I'd be scrambling around—trying to find the keys to the kingdom.

Many times I go to look for something in the pantry and stand gazing, wondering why I opened the door. Although this is a period of life for us to think of the hereafter, I don't think it was intended that we should wander from place to place, wondering what we're 'here after.'

Some say God didn't give older women babies because they'd forget where they put them. That may not only be a problem for older women. I didn't do very well with my own children—when I was young.

When our youngest son, Chip, was three, we visited a church an hour's drive from where we lived. It was an evening service and as had been my custom, I dressed the children for bed before we drove home. We had a pallet in the back of the station wagon where they'd fall asleep and we could slip them in their own beds when we arrived at home.

That night we put them in the car and stood outside to visit with members of the church. Without our knowledge, Chip slid across and crawled out the opposite door and went back to play. We drove away and arrived home late. The phone was ringing as we walked in the door. I answered and the preacher from the church we'd visited said, "We take care of all lost children."

"What?"

"Have you counted your kids? You left one of them in the church yard." I gasped, but before I could answer, he continued. "But listen, why don't you leave him and come back to the meeting tomorrow night? He can wear some of our children's clothes tomorrow."

I was mortified, but I talked to Chip and found he was happy to stay there. We were relieved not to have to turn around and go back that night— an extra hundred mile trip.

When we walked in the building the following evening, the preacher announced, "Here comes Joseph and Mary, back to the temple to get their son." How good it is that God doesn't forget His children. "Can a mother forget the infant at her breast, walk away from the baby she bore? But even if mothers forget, I'd never forget you" (Isa. 49:15 MSG).

§

Visiting my brother-in-law, Charles, I found him grief-stricken over his beloved wife, Sue. She suffers from an advanced stage of Alzheimer's. He took us to the nursing home to see her. I was shocked. Her mind, once a journal filled with detailed facts, appears to have been coated with acid, which has eaten it away. In the process, her memory burned up, and now it's like an ash-heap. I'm afraid when I knock at the door, no one will answer. A whisper tells me, "She doesn't live here anymore."

God's word assures us He will exchange beauty for ashes. I don't understand that. Oh, to be able to view things from God's perspective. "We don't see things clearly. We're squinting in a fog, peering through a mist. But it won't be long before the weather clears and the sun shines bright! We'll see it all then, see it all as clearly as God sees us, knowing him directly just as he knows us" (1 Cor. 13:12 MSG).

All Charles has left are beautiful memories of by-gone days—of the person Sue used to be. He draws from that well and drinks in the good times, the joy and vivaciousness that flowed from her bright mind. Her mind has seemingly dried up inside a shell. Sue's eyes are now blank. If eyes are the windows of her soul, then the soul appears to have vanished, leaving her body stranded here.

Sue no longer acts rationally. Instead, she reacts with frustration. Is she upset because she can no longer access her mind? Sadly, determination is no longer a factor in getting through to the recesses of her thought life.

Are Sue's attempts to run away a desire to go looking for former years, when she knew who she was, who others were, and where she belonged? How unsettling it would be, to be trapped in such a prison of confusion!

Today, as if she were a tiny child, Charles cares for her body—she's even forgotten how to feed herself. For years he kept hoping someday a smile would burst across her face, her eyes would light up and she'd experience a new awakening. Now, that hope eludes him. He's resigned himself to wait for the time of resurrection, when he can hear God say: "I will repay you for the years the locusts have eaten" (Joel 2:25 NIV). Ah, they will have so much catching up to do. The time of this strange separation makes the days weary and long now. He's waiting and suffering, anticipating a time when the Lord will restore all that has been lost. Sometimes he's tempted to pray, "Lord, come quickly."

§

Most articles written about patients with Alzheimer's are about symptoms and progression of the disease. I pray they discover a way to stop or reverse this horrible assault, but for now, I'm deeply concerned about the caregivers. How difficult it must be, when the caretaker must finally place the patient in a home. I'm told of caretakers who have nagging doubts and guilt because they think they could have possibly taken care of their loved one a little while longer. It's alarming to hear that a number of caretakers, determined to continue to keep their mates at home, end up dying before the patient.

As compassionate followers of Christ, it would be good to commit to reach out to these people. I understand that caregivers experience many emotions—such as fears, anger and frustration. Depression, hopelessness and self-pity may follow. Their situation surely must be more difficult than those of us who've experienced the loss of a loved one in death.

A support group can be invaluable for those close to the patient. They lean on each other, especially since they no longer have an understanding spouse in whom they can confide. Those of us who've never experienced their trauma cannot adequately empathize with them.

My prayer is for those of you who care for a loved one in this condition. I pray our Father will give you wisdom each step of the way and give you the strength—to hold steady at a time when every resource in you is being stretched.

How Can We Keep Our Minds Healthy?

It is imperative to keep our minds stimulated by crossword puzzles, Sudoku, research and memorization, though these may not be enough. Challenges to our thinking and physical exercise are helpful. Some medications and vitamins may stall the progression—somewhat.

Passages of scripture tell us we can have the mind of Christ and that our mind can be renewed. I pray these scriptures regularly. Time will tell if this is a deterrent to memory loss. Beyond that, my hope has been relegated to the area of faith and trust.

Memorizing scripture has been proven to strengthen the memory. It has many benefits. It is not only good for our minds—it is good for us spiritually. When I turned seventy-five, I felt a nudging to memorize Jesus' Sermon on the Mount. The idea kept returning to my mind as if it were an urging from the Lord. I resisted. "I can't remember a sentence—much less three chapters of the Bible." Avoidance didn't cause the prompting to go away. Reluctantly, I made three by five note cards with portions of scripture on them. I recorded the sermon to listen to at night as I fell asleep. I copied the recording and kept one in my car and rehearsed verses as I drove.

I reviewed my cards as I waited for doctor's appointments or for the oil to be changed in my car. After three months of memorizing the 111 verses, I was asked to recite them in public on four different occasions. One side benefit was I seldom just sat and stared into space, allowing my mind to play tag with every thought darting through my head. If it is by memorizing scripture or other mind-stimulating activities, we can choose to meditate on the best, not the worst; the beautiful, not the ugly; things to praise, not things to curse. We can focus on joyful and positive thoughts.

§

Even if physical and mental conditions trip us up, we can be assured that as we stay near to God, we'll be in safe hands until we cross the finish line. It will be in His timing. Whatever is missing, malfunctioning or broken will be restored and renewed. For right now, however, we can choose to saturate our minds with God's Word.

We all hope and pray our minds will stay alive as long as our bodies. Regardless of the time and quality of life we've been given, I pray that in every season of life we'll do everything in our power to make it count for God. He helps us redeem whatever time is left.

BE ENTHUSIASTIC

As time slips away, it is easy to lose our enthusiasm. Webster gives the Greek definition of the word 'enthusiasm' as "possession or inspiration of a god." We can be buoyed up with Christ living in us. We're blessed when we find things to be excited about. Enthusiasm usually includes others. Enlist others to join in your excitement. Reach out to people by living outside your immediate circle. God's Holy Spirit can be the motivating force that equips us with the animation to brighten the world around us and encourages us to live outside self-interest.

A friend volunteers to go to a food pantry one day a week to feed the hungry and prepare food baskets to give to the poor. She comes home excited and energized because her actions have made a difference in the lives of others. Another senior, who felt she had no real talents, goes to the nursery at a local hospital to rock preemie babies. The list of possibilities is endless.

When we develop a passion for something, it enlarges our world. My passion at this point is to reach out and offer encouragement to those who are growing older—to plant seeds of optimism that will spur older citizens to carry on through difficult times and make their lives count for something good.

THINGS TO CONSIDER

1. Have you concerns about losing your mental capabilities?

2. Do you have a loved one suffering from some form of dementia?

3. Do you keep active physically, mentally and spiritually?

4. Can you reach out to a caretaker dealing with an Alzheimer's patient?

5. Can you think of doing something you could become passionate about?

6. Have you tried memorizing scriptures to develop your mental abilities?

7. Do you insert challenging things to do into your schedule?

8. List creative ways to stimulate your mind.

9. Write out scriptures you can repeat about the renewal of the mind and having the mind of Christ.

10. Do you stay enthusiastic?

CHAPTER **10**

LOST OPPORTUNITIES

"…when the doors of the street are closed…"

(Eccl.12:4 NIV).

I t's time to quit beating on closed doors and stop looking back. Some doors are permanently locked behind yesterdays. We may not move as fast as we once did, but we can continue to move ahead, looking for other open doors—other opportunities. "It makes no difference who you are or where you're from—if you want God and are ready to do as He says, the door is open" (Acts 10:35 MSG).

§

I don't want to get my hands in the way of any door God may be closing. I was five years old when my sister, "Sis," nineteen years older than I, took the three younger of us children to the circus. Her mother-in-law went along. When we started home, I stood behind the older lady. I had my hand wrapped around the post between the front and back door of the car when she slammed the door on my fingers. I didn't move quickly enough and she opened it and closed it again! In spite of my pain, I was too timid to cry out. Sis turned around and saw tears streaming down my cheeks and said, "Well, what are you crying for? I took you to the circus." I released my pain in a wail and told them what happened. They were mortified. I learned from that accident not to stick my hand in the door when God is ready to close it.

§

A visiting preacher spoke at the church where I went. He begged for us to help his congregation save the retirement home they operated. Funds were inadequate for it to remain open and the resources from members of their church had dried up. The board encouraged members to mortgage their homes in order to keep the doors open. Somehow, this didn't seem right. I approached him after the meeting and asked, "Is it possible that God is trying to tell you it's time to close the doors?" He looked astounded. "We've not even thought about that. Perhaps we do need to make sure this is God's plan, rather than our own."

DOORS BEGIN TO CLOSE

Age sneaked up on my blind side and a door began to close as my health and energy began to wane. The job of running the retreat center, "Hidden Manna," for fifteen years had been a wonderful experience. However, I decided not to wait much longer— as age might begin to affect my ability to cook, clean, and mow. I loved the job, but the time seemed right to slow down. I'd told the board that when I reached 75 it would probably be a good idea for me to step back. They agreed. God turned my attention to aspects of what I was doing that *could* continue—such as counseling, seminars, teaching, mentoring and writing. I'd need to move and be transplanted to another spot. There are risks in transplanting an old, established tree, but I trusted I could still bear fruit in another garden. I packed up most of my personal belongings and put my furniture in storage.

God can use an older person as a caretaker to offer water in the form of encouragement to those who are weary. The world has been compared to fields of ripened grain. God, as the Lord of the harvest, calls for workers to go out and bring in those whose souls are ready to be harvested.

Doors are open in the kingdom for the elderly as well as the young. I see light seeping under a new door that's beginning to crack open. I can minister to those in the new neighborhood where I moved. Jesus leads us to minister in large and small ways—even if it's simply stuffing envelopes at the church office or taking cookies across the street.

God's way may not lead to doors that are large or impressive. Some opportunities may come in the form of leading people to someone that can help them. We can be on the look-out for resources where people can get the help they need—whether it is for counsel, food or money. When we have a peace about a door that appears to be opening, it's often a clue that it's time to move full speed ahead. "But I have learned to feel safe and satisfied, just like a young child on its mother's lap" (Psa. 131:2 CEV). We enjoy great contentment when we're in the center of God's will.

WATCH FOR NEW DOORS TO OPEN

Retirement dismisses us from the mainstream of the work world, where doors are sometimes kicked open by force. Manipulative people have picked the locks to get what they wanted. Those who pursue self-serving ambitions often push, struggle and even step on others to make sure they get through the right doors.

When some retire, they feel unneeded and unfulfilled. Their goals and incentives disappear because they decide their life counts for little now. Discouragement may cause their immune system to falter. With that defense lowered, depression and apathy make them vulnerable to health problems.

God's method is completely different. He opens doors with mustard seed faith and offers vistas greater than we ever dreamed. It is so beautiful when a little faith opens doors that no man can close. Doors hinged on faith are oiled by the Holy Spirit. This causes them to swing wide open.

On a trip to a foreign country as a tourist, I had the opportunity to teach a class in an underground Christian school. The following year I began thinking of possibly going back and teaching for a longer period of time. I dismissed the idea since I'd not had the training to do this type of work. I didn't speak the language and it involved teaching a full five hours a day for a week. It would be difficult and a little scary, but the thought kept circulating through my mind. Finally, I mentioned it to a friend.

This friend called me back the following day and said, "If you decide to go, my husband and I have enough frequent flyer mileage to send you." I was flabbergasted but decided I should at least see if the school needed me. I e-mailed the man in charge and gave him a brief resume. He sent me a return e-mail the following day, stating: "You have been invited to participate in what we believe is one of the most exciting outreaches in the Christian world today." My heart leapt—I'd heard from God.

A lady at church heard of my plans and wrote out a check for a thousand dollars. She said, "I don't want you to be out a dime of your own money."

My niece called me before my second trip the next year and offered to cover all my expenses. When time for the third trip rolled around, several donors provided every cent I needed. It appeared God had not only opened the door, but ushered me through it. Memories of these trips inspire me and stoke dying embers of excitement until they become full-blown flames, drawing me back. While there, I teach the Bible, pray for students and encourage them by sharing my own struggles, victories and defeats. They get excited about what God has planned for their lives.

A Soldier for God

When we enlist in God's army, the enemy waits beside new doors of opportunity. He comes against us, brandishing weapons of fear and doubt. His demons threaten, hoping we'll scramble back into fox holes or the safety of our homes. God's Holy Spirit provides a boldness to go forward with Him—no turning back.

Several asked me, "Aren't you afraid to go to a country that is so opposed to Christianity?" I tell them, "If God commissions me to go, I'm afraid *not* to go."

STAY IN GOOD HEALTH

It's easier to stand tall and walk through the doors God opens if we if we are in good health. We need to eat right and get more vitamin D—especially by being outdoors. This can affect both the length and quality of our lives. Take time to listen to birds, look up at the clouds, trees and God's creation. Find the quiet ebb and flow of nature and absorb its relaxing benefits. All this is vital in staying vibrant and healthy.

Up to this point in time, the emphasis has been on how the world affects us. We can make it a top priority to assess how we can impact the world. God is our CEO (Creator—Everlasting—Omnipotent). We hold our plans up to our Maker and wait for His stamp of approval by opening doors for us.

WATCH THE FOCUS

My sister, Ruth, and her husband, Jim, were driving home after a gathering of other seniors. Ruth remarked: "Jim, it seems like the bulk of time this evening was spent listening to others harp on their ailments and the medications they're on. Let's resolve to never get caught up with grumbling and making our illnesses the main topic of conversation. We need to talk about cheerful things rather than rehearsing our complaints."

Counterfeit creativity can take the form of painting a dismal picture of our lives or our circumstances. Negative attitudes slow down the production of endorphins—the basis of 'feel good' emotions. Negative thinking destroys meaningful creativity.

The enemy plants many thoughts in our minds. While some ideas are our own, we must learn to distinguish thoughts from God, Satan, or ourselves. The Father's thoughts spiral upward in the form of hope, love, peace and joy. Thoughts coming from the enemy spiral downward—negative thoughts of hopelessness, discouragement, grumbling and complaining. Grab these disgusting thoughts and cast them out. "We take captive every thought to make it obedient to Christ" (2 Cor. 10:5 NIV).

Satan wants us to believe we've passed the prime time of our lives and we can no longer be productive. Perhaps if we listen closely, we'll hear God calling us to a different plane. We need to be selective to whom we listen.

Preparing for the Inevitable

Carey had been in the hospital for a week. When the doctor told us there was nothing else they could do, he asked the children and me if he should keep him on life support. I said, "I think he's able to understand you, talk to him." We stood around the bed as the doctor explained the prognosis to Carey. Carey didn't hesitate. He made motions, indicating he wanted the doctor to pull the plugs. The staff did as he directed and Carey was moved to a private room. There, with labored speech, Carey made a recording to be played to the church. He encouraged Christians to praise God more freely in worship.

As visitors came for a last visit, he asked them to tell good stories, to read the Bible and sing to him. He was surrounded with uplifting music, words and actions. Some patted his hands; others rubbed his feet or washed his face with a cool cloth.

The night Carey died, Chip was alone with him in the room. He prayed, "Lord, either heal him or take him." Within minutes, Carey stopped breathing. Chip ran to the desk and told the nurses to call the doctor. He hurried into the waiting room nearby where I was talking with friends and urged me, "Come quickly!" I rushed back and stood on one side of his bed while the doctor stood on the other, taking his pulse. In a few moments she looked at me and said, "He's gone."

I immediately looked up and whispered, "Lord Jesus, receive his spirit," and then turned and spoke sternly, "Satan, you did *not* win; you may have closed one door, but God will open others." I remembered God taught His people to take care of the widows and orphans. I felt confident—there were wonderful people who would help get me though the dark days ahead.

The statement about God opening other doors became a self-fulfilling prophesy. God continued to work in many areas of my life. There were opportunities of teaching, speaking, seminars, ministry and outreach.

Before Carey's death, most of my outreaches involved working with him on seminars, retreats, home Bible studies and entertaining. After he was gone, the transition came slowly. First, I took in an unwed mother to stay with me until her baby was born and adopted. I developed other gifts God had given me. I discovered new ways to touch and change lives.

I obtained a key to the church building and started going there early mornings to pray. One morning I woke up and remembered my daughter-in-law had borrowed that key. I was tempted to roll over and go back to sleep, but felt a strong urge to get up. I mumbled as I dressed and drove to church, "This is useless.

All the doors will be locked." Arriving at the church building, a woman who was a member of the church drove up beside me. No one had ever joined me before. I explained to her about the key, but we decided to check the doors anyway. One *was* open! We went in for an hour of prayer. Neither of us questioned who made arrangements for that door to remain unlocked.

§

When Marie Banister, a godly Christian woman, visited a child in MD Anderson cancer hospital years ago, she took a pretty, soft pillow. When she saw how other children wanted to touch and feel it, she enlisted other women and over the years, they made and gave away over 120,000 pillows to children at the hospital. She worked until her death at eighty-nine. Don't underestimate the value of small ideas that come as an opportunity to reach out to others.

My friend, Joanne, who is in her mid-seventies, has been going to a retaining facility for a number of years— to teach Bible lessons and pray with delinquent teenage girls. She encourages them to believe they can still have successful lives. She gets e-mails and letters from those who return home. Many are making good choices and starting over again.

My brother-in-law, Jim, who at this writing is seventy-nine, has made it his ministry to do odd jobs for widows and single mothers around his community. His services are loved and appreciated by many of us. I asked, "Don't you get tired of doing difficult and dirty jobs?" He grinned and said, "No, not really. It gives me pleasure to know I'm offering a service for those who can't do these things for themselves." He's proof that things we do for ourselves may give us temporary satisfaction, but the things we do for others will leave us with a warm afterglow. He has a true servant's heart. At church they call him a sheep dog—one who helps look after the sheep.

If you've not been involved in reaching out, begin by taking baby steps. As God sees our willingness to be a servant, He opens more and bigger doors of opportunity. I believe Abraham Lincoln knew what he was saying when he commented, "If I prepare myself, perhaps my chance will come."

It is tempting to pamper ourselves by just spending our days playing golf, watching TV, going out to eat or shopping frequently. The bumper sticker "Shop til you drop" seems pointless. We can choose how empty or full our lives are to be. It's easy to become self-centered at any age, but especially when we're older and have more time on our hands.

When I moved into the community where I live, a neighbor asked, "Do you play golf or tennis?"

"No, I don't."

"Do you play bridge?"

I shook my head. "Sorry." When I mentioned this to my daughter-in-law, she said, "Did you tell her you have a life?" Please don't misunderstand me. There is absolutely nothing wrong with any of these activities. But the time spent with things that are just for our own pleasure can easily become the focal point of our lives.

Since most seniors are no longer employed, there's a temptation to get involved in mindless talk and gossip. E-mails and chit chatting on the phone have the potential of being unhealthy traps for any of us to say more than we should. Some become so absorbed in Face book and other social networking sites, they spend the bulk of their time sending messages about almost every move they make. "Set a guard over my mouth, O LORD; keep watch over the door of my lips" (Psa. 141:3 NIV).

If we're willing to follow, God can lead us to unparalleled heights. "By entering through faith into what God has always wanted to do for us—set us right with him, make us fit for him— we have it all together with God because of our Master Jesus. And that's not all: We throw open our doors to God and discover at the same moment that he has already thrown open his door to us" (Rom. 5:2 MSG). The door knob represents a decision—our will is required to open the door.

THE POWER OF ENCOURAGEMENT

When I was being introduced at a retreat, the lady told the audience, "Louise probably saved my life many years ago. She talked to me about how to deal with some emotional problems I wrestled with." I was embarrassed, but I couldn't remember ever meeting the lady. It's incredible how a little encouragement can have a great impact. It's sobering to think that a casual comment could change the course of someone's life.

Our senior citizens may well be Christianity's greatest un-tapped resource. Are some things stirring in your mind yet? Why not be a conduit for God's light to shine through? Many seniors need no financial support and they can offer years of invaluable experience. "It makes no difference who you are or where you're from—if you want God and are ready to do as he says, the door is open" (Acts 10:34-36 MSG).

THINGS TO CONSIDER

1. Have you had a door of opportunity to close on you recently?

2. As you grow older, are you looking for new or different things you can do?

3. What talents or gifts would you like to develop in the future?

4. Name factors you may need to consider in pursuing new goals.

5. Do you think that you're too old to change your habits?

6. Are you watching your diet and exercising to keep yourself in good health?

7. Are you focused too much on yourself and your own desires?

8. Name some negative thoughts that Satan has put in your mind about aging.

9. Are there habits or ruts you need to break out of?

10. Do you have the courage to step out and volunteer in different ways to help others?

CHAPTER 11

THE DAILY GRIND SHUTS DOWN

"...and the sound of the grinding fades..." (Eccl. 12:4 NIV).

THE GRINDING IN THE WORKPLACE SHUTS DOWN

At the office, I'd cleaned out my desk and now sat at the head table for the retirement party. It was then I discovered they were no longer giving away gold watches. Likely, they figured time wouldn't be important to me since I'd no longer be punching a time clock.

My meager retirement benefits caused me to hit the ground—not running, but with a dull thud. There'd be no golden parachute to float leisurely through fluffy clouds for the remainder of my life.

Father Time led me quietly out the door and closed it. The sounds of the work place grew faint. No doubt about it, the daily grind had come to a halt. I knew many viewed this past era of employment as most significant. This seemed to imply everything from now on would be a downhill slide.

111

Along with frustration and self-pity, the workaholic demon in my brain darted about my head, relentlessly whispering, "Retirement is evidence that you're nigh on to useless now."

Animosity moved in to join fellow tormentors. I had to decide whether I'd offer him a cozy warm place to build his nest and hatch his eggs or if I'd knock him out of the way and tell him to go somewhere else to roost. Thankfully, I chose the latter.

The grinding of the workplace involved polishing job skills and sanding off rough edges of poor performance. Then, it wasn't uncommon for the boss to use a hammer and chisel to make sure those edges got knocked off. The emphasis had been on productivity, and that's where we found our significance and value—as underlying ingredients of self-worth. Leaving the workplace can leave an empty void in our lives. It may cause us to feel we're socially dropping out of sight.

GOD AS A SCULPTOR

However, if we're alert, we can find God at work on the inside to make our lives more about *who* we are rather than *what* we do. The Father carefully focuses on us as 'human beings' rather than 'human doings'. In a whole new way His emphasis is on grinding off the rough edges of the inner man.

In many ways, the process God uses to shape us is not unlike that of a sculptor. He takes potentially good raw material and begins to chisel away everything that doesn't enhance the work of art He envisions. Chunks are chiseled off our lives as the Lord works on areas of pride. Selfishness is chopped away as He shapes us so we'll fit into His plan. Ouch!

It takes time, some of which is painful, but the Lord is tenacious and patient in creating a masterpiece. We have the option to resist and not become a work of art—but if we choose that option—we'll miss the touch of the Master's hand.

Our stubborn wills are like rock. The One who shapes our lives is intent on grinding away every resistant attitude. We're tempted to pull away from God and hang on to our hard-hearted ways. But hopefully, we'll reconsider and yield to His touch, allowing Him to grind away those bad traits until they become like sand and filter out of our lives.

§

Chip, my son, had a rebellious streak as a teen. To say his lifestyle was unacceptable is an understatement. Once he disappeared for three months before coming back into our lives. I prayed for him for a number of years, seemingly to no avail. I kept telling God, "I want to turn him over to You, but please don't hurt Chip." Finally, in desperation, I prayed aloud, "God, regardless of what You have to do, bring someone or something into his life that will turn him around."

A couple of weeks later Chip called, "My friend and I went camping at Lake Dallas. A couple of bums came up with knives and robbed us. I had every penny to my name in my wallet. As soon as they left, my buddy suggested we jump in my van to try to catch them—to get close enough to get their license number. In the process, we skidded around a corner on the gravel road and rolled the van. I crashed through the windshield into the pathway of an oncoming car. In a dazed state, I raised my hand to

113

plead, "God don't let them hit me." The car screeched to a stop and they called for an ambulance to come take me to the hospital to be sewn up. I'm at Rick's (his brother) house. Mom, could you come get me?"

Carey and I drove to Dallas to pick him up and bring him home. Afterwards, we went to the police pound to check on his van. It was crushed like a Styrofoam cup, not worth the price of bailing it out. We drove back to Houston with very little conversation.

The following Sunday, Chip went to church with us. I overheard him talking to some of the young people. "God knew what He had to do to get my attention."

This incident jump-started a one hundred and eighty degree turn in his life. He not only made a recommitment to the Lord but went deeper—to make God his number one priority. Now, years later, he and his wife are a gifted praise and worship team at church.

As a loving father, Chip beams with pride over his daughters. He smiles, "I always dreamed of being surrounded by beautiful women, but never realized it would come true through my wife and three beautiful little girls."

When God chiseled chunks off his life it was painful, but I'm convinced—the Father wouldn't have used dynamite if a firecracker would have done the job. "Thank You, Lord, you are a wise and dynamic force, intent on changing lives." Interestingly, it usually requires that we get our hands off a situation before He takes over.

IRON SHARPENS IRON

God seems to allow us to be in close proximity with at least one person who grinds on our nerves. God brought someone to live with me who exposed many of my negative traits. Our personalities clashed. She was serious while I was flippant. By nature, she was super-organized—I was not.

Both of us loved the Lord, so we should have gotten along great, right? Wrong. She took it upon herself to be responsible to watch over me and *help* me. Buzzing around in the kitchen with my 'type A' personality, she corrected and cautioned me: "Use a pot holder to lift that skillet—it's hot. Did you wash the pinto beans before you put them on to cook? Be careful and don't fall when you go down the steps." I stuffed my feelings and gritted my teeth as these things continued to grind on my nerves.

In her attempts to help, I felt smothered and manipulated. Irritation kindled a fire within until one day, I lashed out, "I don't need you as a mother, standing over me to watch and monitor everything I do. Thank you very much. I'm past sixty-five and managed quite well for decades before you ever came along." She retaliated by writing me a scathing letter, listing the grievances she had against me.

There'd been too little application of Biblical principles in my life. I read the Word daily, but if you'd asked me what I read about, I might have answered, "About fifteen minutes." "You have your heads in your Bibles constantly because you think you'll find eternal life there. But you miss the forest for the trees. These scriptures are all about me! And here I am standing right before you, and you aren't willing to receive from me the life you say you want" (Jn. 5:39-40 Msg.).

I considered suggesting this lady and I go our separate ways, but then we decided to start each day by reading a brief segment of the Bible together, journaling and asking God what He would say to us that day. God didn't hesitate to point out a number of flaws in each of us. We shared our thoughts every morning and prayed together.

Changes began to evolve. Before, our lives had been a tiny flicker of light rather than a beacon on a hill. God used the grinding process to polish our rough edges. We welcomed the day when the sound of our grumbling and grinding began to fade.

This common practice developed a long-lasting friendship which permitted the two of us to reach out together in ministering to others. We minimized our differences. We set boundaries and worked out a division of chores. Our interactions ran more smoothly.

The heavy tenseness began to lift. We included guests in our daily devotionals and they also felt free to talk about their own personal struggles. As we shared and applied God's Word, He began a process of refining those of us who took part in the venture. It was a beautiful experience—we'd decided to let God polish us up before He polished us off.

A friend suggested, "Look past your surroundings here and reach out to others. You'll learn to please God by pleasing others." This suggestion provoked serious considerations. We wanted our lives to count for something, and yes, to be needed. We searched for spiritual gifts that had lain dormant. In our heart of hearts, we knew it wasn't too late for God to use us.

I determined to look beyond the barbecue grill in the back yard and past the flat screen television in the living room. Volunteer work surrounded us. It felt good to spend time in the prayer rooms, go on mission trips and take food to the sick. We both zeroed in on things that we could make right in the world, rather than focus on the things that were wrong in our immediate surroundings.

§

Ah yes, we had time to read more than usual. We decided to become better acquainted with the Bible. A scripture in Revelation intrigued us. It spoke of those who stand before God throughout eternity, repeating, "Holy, Holy, Holy, Lord God Almighty, who was and is and is to come." We concluded it could be compared to looking at a giant disco ball. Each time one looked up, he'd discover a new and magnificent virtue of God's goodness. Facet after shining facet would reflect His brilliance and majesty. We realized we could marvel over Jehovah God forever, without growing weary. This proved to be an incentive for us to spend more time praising God for His innumerable attributes.

Our Later Years may be our Best Years

It's strange how God sometimes waits until the evening shadows of life begin to fade before fulfilling His greatest purposes through his children. God sent Abraham back to square one during his old age. He had him begin populating the world with His chosen people when he was almost a hundred years old. I'd like to say, "Lord, choose me," but I don't want to be like Sarah and have a baby at this stage of the game. Shiver me timbers!"

God literally put Moses 'out to pasture' for forty years before calling him to his greatest assignment. Some say the apostle Paul was not ready to be used by God until he was made a 'basket case' and lowered down over the wall in a basket and dropped out of sight for several years. No doubt He has plans to use us for as long as we can totter along.

A remarkable number of people make their greatest contribution late in life. Mary Frances, an older woman at church, had retired after teaching at a local University. She busied herself throughout the community by becoming involved in all kinds of activities. She volunteered to help with benevolent causes and staffed the prayer room every week. She commented in the midst of all her involvement, "I just wish I could do more."

The doctors discovered Mary Frances had cancer, but she kept going until they insisted she go into the hospital. When the preacher visited her, she demanded, "You have to get me out of here, I have too much to do." She died the following day at age eighty-nine. I suppose God thought she was talking to Him, so He obliged her—and got her out of there! Most of the people in the city knew her because of the number of lives she'd touched. She'd been elected Woman of the Year shortly before her death. Her determination to go out and help others never came to a grinding halt. How good to know someone who lives such a full life.

§

Since the sounds of the grinding of the work-place have 'grown low', it's time to step aside and ask God to lead and polish us. "Calling the crowd to join his disciples, he said, 'Anyone who intends to come with me has to let me lead. You're not in the driver's seat; I am" (Mk. 8:34 MSG).

When we yield to God's deliberate touch, it's not a meaning-less grinding away of time, but a time to allow him to work on each aspect of our lives until an exquisite sculpture is complet-ed. It requires perseverance to live under the masterful touch of God's care. "We pray that you'll have the strength to stick it out over the long haul—not the grim strength of gritting your teeth but the glory-strength God gives. It is the strength that endures the unendurable and spills over into joy, thanking the Father who makes us strong enough to take part in everything bright and beautiful that he has for us" (Col. 1:11-12 MSG).

ME—CREATIVE?

Creativity is a motivating factor that inspires us to come up with great new ideas. A church invited me to speak at their weekend retreat for a group of about 250 women. With that in mind, I began to prepare my materials. I kept thinking of skits that would illustrate the lessons I wanted to teach. Though in my sixties, I'd never acted before—except in small high school plays. But I decided to conduct the whole retreat, using drama. That stretched my creativity.

The first night I dressed in costume. Right before going onstage, panic hit. *Oh dear, there're probably many actresses in the audience and quite possibly some who even teach drama.* I trembled, my heart pounded and my mouth went dry. Suddenly, deep within, the Lord whispered, "If you're afraid, it's either because you don't think I've given you the talent to do this, you missed my leading or you want to impress the audience. None of these excuses is acceptable."

I swallowed hard. "Forgive me, Lord, I'm ready—front and center." All of a sudden, it didn't matter if the people thought I was good or not. I would be obedient to what God led me to do. As a result, God used the skits powerfully to change lives—in spite of my amateurish presentation.

We probably all have creativity relegated to a back shelf of our minds—asleep for years—waiting to be awakened. Come on, Grandma Moses—if it's art, invite it to come out. Creativity can be in many forms: knitting, playing an instrument or developing a hobby—anything that inspires new talents or develops old ones. Some find sign language a creative way of expression. Scratch your head, there's something itching to come out. Better still, ask God for suggestions.

The Master's work of chiseling and grinding, sandpapering and polishing, are a part of the transformation process. We can refuse to get bogged down in the daily grind of living by asking God, "Help us be more creative."

COULD WE BE DIAMONDS IN THE ROUGH?

Stories are told about the finding and cutting of the Hope Diamond. The most skilled diamond cutter in the world was commissioned for the task. They gave him the rough diamond and he kept it for a year—looking at it, touching it, turning it over and over to discover the best approach in order to reflect its exquisite beauty and size. His meticulous skill allowed him to cut this magnificent stone. I'd like to think God is watching us— waiting until He's sure we're ready to hold still on the work table. Then He'll smooth off the rough edges so we can become something of great value.

God has, no doubt, been chipping on our rough edges for years. Perhaps He's ground off most of the coarse places and can start polishing us now as He puts on the finishing touches. "The Lord their God will save them on that day as the flock of his people. They will sparkle in his land like jewels in a crown. How attractive and beautiful they will be!" (Zech. 9:16-17 NIV)

So here we are—diamonds in the rough. God would have us be so transparent that Jesus' reflection can be seen from every angle, every facet. He wants to place us where we'll catch the light of the Son. "I made you grow like a plant of the field. You grew up and developed and became the most beautiful of jewels" (Ezek. 16:7 NIV). Someday, I want to end up in God's jewelry box.

It's time to pray for a faith that will deepen our dependence on God, to create a sparkling and abundant life. Let me invite you along with Robert Browning, "Grow old along with me, the best is yet to be."

THINGS TO CONSIDER

1. What can you do to keep retirement from making you feel unimportant?

2. Do you have conflicting feelings about leaving the workplace?

3. Is God working on any rough edges of your life?

4. Since many of us are free from making a living, are you ready to look for new priorities in life?

5. Do you read the Bible and journal—write about the struggles you are facing now?

6. Think of someone who has remained active in life.

7. Name some of those who may be watching how you live your life.

8. Do you ever make excuses that keep you from doing something new or different?

9. Are there areas of creativity you could develop?

10. How might we, at our age, become valuable to those around us?

CHAPTER 12

WAKE ME WHEN IT'S TIME FOR BED

"…when men rise up at the sound of birds…" (Eccl. 12:4 NIV).

One of the benefits of growing older is that we don't need a jangling alarm to get us up at the crack of dawn to go to work. Our jobs no longer call our names. So, what happens when we go into retirement? Our eyes pop open before daylight, and twist and turn as we might, we can't get back to sleep. We unwittingly become an early bird. So much for the fact we never cared much for worms! A little saying I remember from childhood makes me smile, "Tis spring and the birdies peep, I wish they'd shut up and let me sleep."

However, rather than chirping birds being an irritation, I decided to enjoy them and consider them to be a wake-up call singing, "Welcome to my world." Perhaps in bird language they're announcing, "This is the day that the Lord has made, let us rejoice and be glad in it" *(Psa. 118:24 NIV)*. Listen carefully, one bird seems to be calling, "Cheer-ee, Cheer-ee, Cheer-ee."

The mood we wake up with may well stay with us throughout the day. That well-worn expression about people getting up on the wrong side of the bed contains a lot of truth. But happily, we have a choice as to how we hit the floor in the morning. We take control of our thoughts so our minds won't flip back to yesterday's struggles or to skip ahead to today's concerns. It's helpful to remember to ask God for guidance and trust Him to orchestrate the best plans for us—each day.

If it's our desire to wake up to the sound of a bird, let's pick a cheerful one to emulate. Let their warbles lift our spirits from early morning until we hit the pillow at night. "So you will go out with joy, you'll be led into a whole and complete life. The mountains and the hills will lead the parade, bursting with song. All the trees of the forest will lead the procession, exuberant with applause" (Isa. 55:12 Msg.). Be refreshed. Go outside and soak up the joy of the Creator's great outdoors. Since God infused joy in all creation, let it be a mandate for us to sing praise as nature does. Pretend joy is like a treasure hidden in the field and we're excited about going out and digging for it.

AMBASSADORS OF JOY

I believe God sent birds as ambassadors of joy—instruments of praise. Because of our name, some refer to us as "Looney birds." My son, Paul, is a psychiatrist and is teased about his name—a shrink named Looney. My younger son, Chip, owns a music store, so you can imagine what kind of tunes he's accused of playing. We've committed to join the rest of the songbirds in a chorus of praise.

Before Paul sent his son off to kindergarten, he explained to him that others might make fun of his name because the word 'looney' often implies that a person is crazy. His son, Adam, came home a few days later and announced, "I know why our name is Looney. It's because we're crazy about each other."

§

Falling Asleep at the Wrong Times

As people grow older, there's often a problem of waking up early and falling asleep at inappropriate times. Many older citizens quite regularly fall asleep during the nightly ten o'clock news. They miss the weather report they stayed up to watch. I'm not sure that's essential to know, since many of us don't have an agenda the weather would affect. However, the bits and pieces of news we do catch enable us to put in our two cents worth when we're dawdling around and talking with other seniors. If we don't pick up a little news, how will we be able to solve the world's problems?

I've fallen asleep watching a movie and ended up missing the ending. That's disgusting. Oh well, I might as well stretch and engage in a long, noisy yawn, brush my teeth and go to bed. In a couple of days, I won't remember the movie anyway.

All Creation Expresses Joy

A baby's smile plays a role in the bonding process—compensating for the dirty diapers and rocking him during the wee hours of the night when he has colic. Nothing thrills a new mom, dad or grandparent more than those first smiles. It's also fun to watch a doting father make all kinds of weird faces and gyrations in an attempt to get the baby to smile again. Some claim a smile is the first sign of a baby's intelligence. As a person ages, it may not indicate intelligence, but it may well be evidence of wisdom. I wonder—could it be that our laughter and smiles are a part of the bonding process with our Father?

Even before God woke up man at the foundation of the world, He sprinkled joy, like dew, across His Creation. No doubt He sat back with deep satisfaction and watched it sing and clap its hands. "Let the fields be jubilant, and everything in them. Then all the trees of the forest will sing for joy" (Psa. 96:12 NIV).

Imagine all creation being infused with joy and bowing down before His throne. The heavens, blanketed with stars, are singing praises to God while angels shout their loudest praise. Surely the heavens must continue to radiate with laughter and burst forth in song. "Who supports the foundation? Who placed the cornerstone, while morning stars sang and angels rejoiced?" (Job 38:6-7 CEV).

When God birthed the earth, I'm confident that as He spoke each element into existence, it responded by giving glory to the Creator for His masterful craftsmanship. We too, rejoice in Him. "On your feet now—applaud God! Bring a gift of laughter, sing yourselves into his presence" (Psa. 100:1-2 MSG). We're told God inhabits the praises of His people. This gives us an opportunity to come into His throne-room.

Look at nature and experience God's waterfall of love. We lift our hands to accept all the gifts He showers on His children. Rivers of love cascade down from the hills and inspire us to sing with all of nature.

Peace and joy reign in our hearts when we accept that He's perfectly capable of handling everything that happens today. If He numbers the hairs of our head—even when they're a tangled mess, surely He's concerned for our lives when they are messy and tangled.

The swallow teaches us a lesson as we observe the place he builds his nest. Scripture tells us that sparrows and swallows make their nests near God's altars. We're invited to come near and nest peacefully in His presence.

Joy is an essential element in staying young. We invite peace and joy to be our traveling companions while walking these last miles. Life is not only enhanced, but flourishes in the presence of these two friends.

The Benefits of Laughter

Even secular research proves that laughter can heal diseases, decrease pain and contribute to building a stronger immune system. A number of years ago, Norman Cousins did extensive research on the biochemistry of human emotions. He brought this to the world's attention with his own personal experiment.

Cousins had been given little chance of surviving an illness when he implemented a recovery program that combined mega doses of vitamin C with laughter. He watched funny movies and read books and jokes that made him laugh. These tactics became a major factor in his battle to live. He included a positive attitude, love, faith and hope. He concluded that ten minutes of genuine belly laughter had an anesthetic effect and would give

127

him at least two hours of pain-free sleep. (*The Anatomy of an Illness as Perceived by the Patient*, New York: Norton, 1979)

FIND JOY IN THE PRESENCE OF GOD

I suspect praise and joy can swing open the gates that lead into the presence of God. Joy makes the journey through life so much easier. Our steps are energized and burdens become lighter when joy skips along beside us.

In order to make room for joy, sweep out complaining and pessimism, lest we track dirt all over the place. We come into the throne-room to receive our booster shot of joy for the day. The world gives us no comparable substitute. How wonderful it is that God's presence builds our immune system against grumpiness.

Joy is one of the gifts of the Holy Spirit. It is a small word with great meaning. As children, we were taught the word *joy* stood for **J**esus first, **O**thers second, and **Y**ourself last. This is possibly the shortest route to experiencing happiness at the core of our being.

My husband, a psychologist, conducted a number of seminars. When he spoke, he often used me as the brunt of his jokes. This was one of his favorites: "Someone asked me if I woke up grumpy every day, and I told them, 'No, sometimes I let her sleep late.'

One day a woman approached me after a lecture and questioned me, "How can you stand hearing him talk about you the way he does?" I chuckled, "If I laugh louder than anyone else, everyone will think he's teasing and believe the things he says about me are not really true."

§

When I think of a delightful bird, the bluebird comes to mind. Some refer to it as the bluebird of happiness. Bluebirds are meticulous. They build their nests at a specific height. Watching them sail through the air brings me pleasure. We invite them to sit on our shoulder and accompany us throughout the day.

The beauty of God's creation reflects the nature of His heart. As we share the gospel of Jesus, we have the opportunity to bring joy into the lives of others. It makes us eligible for our feet to be blessed, because we bring good news. "And how will anyone go and tell them without being sent? That is why the Scriptures say, "How beautiful are the feet of messengers who bring good news!" (Rom. 10:15 NLT)

Isn't it encouraging when we see the first robin after a long, hard winter? That bird announces that the hope that spring is on its way. We love to be around people who remind us that God is on His way—with good things planned for this new season of our lives. We appreciate those who encourage us to look beyond present circumstances—to the time when our burdens will be lifted after a long, hard winter of trials. If we approach God with our requests, sandwiched between praise, might He not be pleased to answer those prayers?

It is striking that God used a dove to deliver the message to Jesus—that He loved him as His Son and He was well pleasing in His sight. The sound of a dove is one of the most soothing of bird songs. Their mellow cooing is relaxing and reassures us, 'all is right with the world.'

The dove is the symbol of peace throughout the world. This idea originated when Noah sent a dove from the ark. The first time the bird flew back to him, but the second time it returned with an olive branch in its beak, indicating it was safe to leave the ark and return to solid ground. We love to be around those who make us feel peaceful. We feel comfortable in their presence. Jesus promises this kind of peace. "I am leaving you with a gift—peace of mind and heart, and the peace I give is a gift the world cannot give. So don't be troubled or afraid" (John 14:27 NLT).

During the early throes of cancer, my husband came out of a store to find a dove perched on the hood of his car. He reached out and the dove hopped in his hand for a brief moment. Though Carey did not receive his healing here, the dove appeared as a special emissary for him—to assure him of God's presence throughout the challenging months ahead.

It's good for most of us to 'get up with the chickens'—to read, journal and pray. Then, we're less likely to be interrupted with visitors or phone calls. Jesus set the example by rising early in the morning—to go to a quiet place to pray while it was still dark. If that fulfilled a need for Him, how much more do we need to rise early to meet with God?

FIND TIME TO SPEND ALONE WITH GOD

However, each person should find his or her own best time to spend alone with the Lord. The enemy often attempts to interrupt this special communion with God. It is wise to take precautions, so we'll not be distracted by anything less than an earthquake. The rewards are great. "I love them that love me; and those that seek me early shall find me" (Prov. 8:17 KJV).

Look for a quiet place to pray. I understand the mother of Charles and John Wesley spent time with the Lord daily. When she threw her apron over her head, all her eighteen children knew she was not to be bothered. Even an apron can be a prayer closet!

Let me encourage you to make a commitment to bring joy into your own life and the lives of those around you. There's a whole new day for us to conquer. Join the cheerful sounds of birds early in the morning. What better way to stay young at heart and be like the birds—by becoming God's ambassadors of joy?

THINGS TO CONSIDER

1. When you can't sleep, are there worthwhile activities you can do?

2. How long has it been since you sat outside to listen to the birds and sounds of nature?

3. Do you make a conscious effort to stay in a good mood throughout the day?

4. Have you smothered joy by grumbling and complaining?

5. Do you believe God intended for our lives to be joyful?

6. Can being joyful help you remain healthy?

7. Do you take time to praise God for His wondrous creation?

8. Do people enjoy being around you because you are pleasant?

9. Name various birds and good attributes you'd like to mimic.

10. Do you have a special time to spend alone with God?

CHAPTER 13

SPEAK UP! I CAN'T HEAR YOU

"...and all their songs grow faint..." (Eccl. 12:4 NIV).

Sounds growing faint are a metaphor for older people with hearing loss. My sister, Ruth, got hearing aids after she discovered she sometimes missed what her grandchildren were saying. After getting the hearing aids, she told her husband, "You know, Jim, you aren't mumbling as much as you did."

Jim smiled. "True, and I'm not forced to talk half as much as I did."

Big Ears and Large Noses

I don't quite understand why older people's ears and noses keep growing as they age. I've surmised that possibly ears flapping farther outside one's head might capture sound waves and help people hear better. But surely big noses aren't an indication that some of us need to smell better!

§

It's sad that the song in some seniors' hearts grows faint when age tromps on them. I'm convinced it's not God's intention that we lose our sense of humor. The joy in our hearts needs to continue to swell as we mediate on His provisions.

Sammie was in a prayer group and had just gone through a divorce. She'd declared bankruptcy and moved from a $600,000 home to a shed in her brother's back yard with no bath room or even a kitchenette. Only a few months later she was diagnosed with breast cancer and scheduled for a double mastectomy. Sammie calmly told the group, "I've never been more at peace." She smiled, "I've always wanted a breast reduction, but hadn't thought of getting this drastic! But guess what? I get to choose the size I want to be." Our eyes widened and our mouths dropped open as we sat amazed at how completely she'd put her life, her faith and trust in God. She's a prime example of how one can hear God's comforting voice in tumultuous times.

A few weeks later, Sammie shared that she'd gone in for tests and locked her heirloom jewelry in a box. When she returned home, the jewelry was gone. Sammie estimated the jewelry was worth over twenty thousand dollars. It disturbed her, but she surmised, "I didn't wear it much and when I did, I was always afraid someone would knock me in the head and steal it. I don't have to worry about that anymore." I marveled. She sincerely believes that things are not really that important.

§

One of my friends went through a devastating trauma when her husband of eighteen years announced he'd filed for divorce.

He'd found a sweet, young thing at the office. Unfortunately, my friend had never worked outside the home, because they'd decided she should be a stay-at-home mom. They had two teenagers. "Not to worry," her husband said, "you can keep the house (with a large mortgage payment) and I'll send you $500 a month to live on." She was devastated as she watched him drive away in a new BMW convertible. There's no way she could make the mortgage payments or raise the children on the pittance he offered. Immobilized, she went into deep depression. She sold the house for just enough equity to buy a small mobile home.

One morning, while reading the Scripture, she came across the following: "A cheerful heart is good medicine, but a crushed spirit dries up the bones" (Prov. 17:22 NIV). She gasped, "I don't want dry bones!" She slinked into her bedroom, closed the door, put on praise and worship music and stood reaching toward the ceiling. In spite of her devastation, she recited, "Praise. . .you. . .Jesus. . . hallelujah. Thank You. . .Lord." She repeated this over and over, until after a time, her shoulders began to lift and she spoke louder and more confidently. Within an hour, she was almost shouting, "Praise you, Jesus. Thank You, Lord. Hallelujah. I know you will get me through this!"

The phone rang. A friend was calling. "You sound so upbeat; did your husband come back?"

"No, he didn't come back, but I've been talking and listening to my heavenly Father and He assured me, "I will never leave you." She went on to explain the miracle happened because she began to praise God as she released the situation to Him. Slowly, she began to rise above the circumstances. She found a job and worked until she made a salary she could live on.

Her children are grown now, but you can always spot her coming with a glowing countenance and a smile on her face. She has remarried and she's well cared for. It is evident— the song in her heart has not grown faint.

I heard others talking about God speaking to them, so I prayed, "Lord, why don't you speak to me?" Deep in my spirit I felt He said, "I'm speaking to you all the time, but you're not listening. I speak through my Word, others, in nature and circumstances. Listen carefully, because sometimes I whisper in a still, small voice."

§

A new challenge may rise up that appears too difficult to handle. Perhaps it's a health issue, a financial problem or most any circumstance that blindsides us. In order to get past it, we're compelled to look higher—to God. I believe He intends for us to listen for His wise counsel at every juncture of our lives. "I look up to the mountains; does my strength come from the mountains? No, my strength comes from God, who made heaven, and earth, and mountains" (Psa. 121:1-3 MSG).

Years ago, I prayed for happiness and a sense of humor. It was as if He anointed me with the oil of joy. Laughter became a natural outburst. There were times when the devil tried to steal that joy, but the Lord stood by me. I refused to let go. Joy accompanies me—even in difficult times. It doesn't mean I'm never sad, but when I make mistakes or things go wrong, I can choose to be the first to find something related to the situation that I can laugh about. Humor combats negative attitudes. I listen to the wisdom Solomon offered about the Proverb's woman: "She is clothed with strength and dignity; she can laugh at the days to come" (Proverbs 31:25 NIV).

I'm convinced God revealed His sense of humor when He put my DNA together. For years, every time we moved to a new city, I'd determine to come across as having it all together with sophistication and poise. This usually lasted approximately five minutes before I'd do or say something weird or dumb. If I laughed first, however, others often ended up laughing and liking me anyway.

I prayed, "God, what is my purpose in life—why did you create me?" I felt He smiled and said, "Bring joy to my heart." I hope I do that on a regular basis. He certainly has brought joy to my heart.

§

I fretted about a relationship problem my son was dealing with. I had difficulty sleeping because of the stress. In a dream, I saw myself in the kitchen stepping in something sticky. I couldn't see anything on the floor. After about the third time stepping in it, my son came in the kitchen and pointed down at a wad of chewing gum and apologized. "I'm sorry, Mom, that's my gum; I'll clean it up."

The impact of this revelation shook me. I confessed. I had continued to step in a sticky situation that was neither my problem nor my responsibility. At the suggestion of another, I chose to step back and spend quality time in prayer—to say less and pray more. The Lord does a much better job scrubbing the glue off sticky situations, so there's no need for me to get stuck in other people's business. I want to learn to listen when God speaks through circumstances and other people.

Look for the Good

A young mother was having a miserable day. She hadn't dressed or combed her hair. The kids were fighting and throwing their toys across the living room. Unfolded clothes were piled high on the couch.

The doorbell rang. She opened the door and gasped when she saw her old boyfriend and his new bride standing there—dressed to a ten with every hair in place.

She hesitantly invited them in as she ran her fingers through her uncombed hair. She stammered an apology for the condition of the house and attempted to carry on an intelligent conversation. The couple visited for a few minutes and left. She was mortified down to her chipped painted toenails and trembled as she dialed her husband at work. After she explained the horrible experience, her husband paused and then said, "Honey, that's wonderful."

She screamed into the phone. "What are you talking about—I can't think of much of anything more humiliating!"

"Wait baby, listen to me. That old boyfriend will never be sorry about the choice he made. His wife will never be jealous of you and last of all—I love you—just the way you are. I'll be home early, honey, and we'll go out to eat."

She cradled the phone and stood there sobbing with gratitude. She called the children in and hugged each of them tenderly. Together, they picked up the toys and put them back in the box. It was time to get a cup of coffee from the kitchen go back to the couch to fold clothes and count her blessings.

Keeping Joy Deep Inside

All the staff had gone to town. It was late in the afternoon when I noticed an orange glow through the window shade. I opened the door and discovered flames of fire from the barn, licking the branches of the tall pine trees behind it. I rushed to call 911 and grabbed a small fire extinguisher and ran toward the flames. I imagined God smiling and whispering, "That's like trying to kill an elephant with a fly swatter!" I threw the extinguisher down and ran quickly to try to get the tractors, riding lawn mowers and golf carts out of the fiery trap.

As I neared the entry, cans of gasoline began to explode. I stopped short. It was too late to risk going inside. "Thank you Lord. You stopped me from rushing in. You likely saved my life."

By the time the fire department arrived, there was nothing left to salvage. The firefighters stayed for hours, continuing to put out fires that kept popping up from the bales of hay stacked at the back of the barn. Dark skeletons of tractors and equipment mocked me as a voice within whispered, "It's gone, *all* gone."

As the staff returned home, we hugged and cried. Paul, our director, suggested we gather in the living room of the main house. He explained, "Fire is often used as a sign of purification. Let's pray that if there's anything unclean in our lives, God will speak to us, so we can confess and repent." He paused. "And remember, our purpose in being here is not dependent on how nice the place looks. If we have to mow a path to the front door with a push mower, we'll do that. Let's pledge to keep our focus on God and what He commissioned us to do—to reach out to hurting people with the healing touch of Jesus."

The five little boys, who were children of the staff, had been in an adjoining bedroom praying. Adam, the oldest, came in with a cross-stitched picture in his hand. "I think we need to hang this where we can see and remember what it says." The Scripture read, "And we know that God causes everything to work together for the good of those who love God and are called according to his purpose for them" (Rom. 8:28 NLT). Hugs and tears thanked him for this reminder.

When I called the insurance company, the agent told me he didn't think any part of our loss was covered, but he would send an insurance adjuster out to look at the damage. A staff member asked, "Louise, how does all this make you feel?"

"I'm sad on the outside, but deep within, there's still a joy."

We released the problem and determined to move on. Re-markably, God showed up. The insurance adjuster came and assured us, "Of course it's covered. In fact, Paul paid extra insurance to include replacement value."

A few months later, we sponsored a barbeque for the purpose of an old fashioned 'barn raisin.' Men brought families and tools. My son, Chip, and his friends furnished live music. By the end of the day, great strides had been made in rebuilding the barn. Our spirits soared. We called it our 'barn again' experience.

WE MAKE CHOICES

Years ago, we moved into an unfinished house in Valparaiso, Indiana. We hired an older gentleman to complete the work. He constantly sang and whistled as he sawed, hammered and painted. One day, I felt it would be good to let him know I'd noticed.

"Joe*, you're a joy to have around. Your singing and whistling are so upbeat."

He turned to me with a solemn expression. "It hasn't always been this way. Twenty years ago my wife and three children were coming into town. When they crossed a railroad track, they were hit by a train. All four of them were killed."

Joe laid down his hammer. "I fell into the depths of depression. I couldn't eat or sleep and couldn't talk about anything else. At the end of six months, a friend put his arm around my shoulder and said, 'Joe, you have been through an incredible tragedy. I don't know what I'd do if I were in your shoes. You may well be depressed for the rest of your life.' He paused and then added, 'I'm sorry, my friend, but I don't think you have the right to make everyone around you miserable.' I was shocked, but his words sank deep into my heart. This man revealed something I needed to hear."

He paused to take a sip of water. "I began to force myself to talk of other things," he continued. "I learned to whistle and began to sing. An ugly scar remains on my heart, but I began to live again." "The Lord is my strength and my song; He has given me victory" (Psa. 118:14 NLT).

Shortly afterwards, we moved to a west Texas town. A couple who were in their seventies went to church where we did. They always looked miserable. One day I asked a member, "What is their problem? They look so downcast—I'll bet when they drink water, it runs out of the down-turned corners of their mouths."

My friend shook her head, "Long ago, their two children were walking home from school after a flash flood. When they started across a bridge, it washed out and they both drowned. This couple became stuck in their grief. It continues to be the dominating factor in their lives."

The difference in how people handle their grief is profound. These examples made a deep impression. I realized we have choices as to how we react to calamities. It's almost a life or death choice. We must determine to never let circumstances muffle the song in our hearts. "By day the Lord directs his love, at night His song is with me" (Psa. 42:8 NIV).

Singing and praise music were often sent ahead of the children of Israel, before they went into battle. Musicians led the way as they affirmed, "The battle belongs to the Lord." When Paul and Silas sang and prayed in prison, God showed His approval by unlocking the prison doors. We need to be aware of situations that may keep us locked behind doors of sadness.

It's disheartening to see people growing old and losing their joy and optimism. I believe in the adage of 'what goes around comes around.' If we take time to send out showers of joy, an abundance of happiness will surely begin to rain down on our own lives. We make a choice to keep the songs of triumph from growing faint in our hearts. "The Lord your God is with you; he is mighty to save. He will take great delight in you, he will quiet you with his love, he will rejoice over you with singing" (Zeph. 3:17 NIV).

Listen carefully—God's insight and wisdom can teach us how to defeat the devil. We become more like Jesus as we listen for the voice of God standing behind us and speaking, "This is the way, walk in it" (Isa. 30:21 NIV).

THINGS TO CONSIDER

1. Does a hearing loss limit your interaction with others?

2. What does joy in the heart do for a person—as well as those around them?

3. What can you do to lift your spirit when you're feeling discouraged?

4. Do we have a choice to stay pleasant and cheerful?

5. Is it hypocritical to force yourself to act happy when you don't feel like it?

6. Can you stay optimistic in spite of tragedies in your life?

7. Think of someone who chose to be cheerful even after tragedies hit them.

8. Think of the contrasts of ways people respond when they encounter difficulties.

9. Do you have praise and worship music that will lift your spirit?

10. Do you know of someone who let a tragedy ruin their whole life?

CHAPTER 14

GET OFF THE LADDER

"...when men are afraid of heights..." (Eccl. 12:5 NIV).

Unless your name is George H.W. Bush, I doubt many will be parachuting from an airplane at age eighty. Heights are usually threatening to older citizens because of their lack of stability, balance and slower reflexes. Our support system of bones is brittle and easily broken. A fall could well mark the end of mobility. "When my skin sags and my bones get brittle, God is rock firm and faithful" (Psa. 73:25 MSG).

An eighty-four- year-old man at church fell and broke his hip. The doctor told his wife, "It's quite possible he won't live another year." Because the man had been active in raising a prize garden and working in the yard, he had firm muscles. As a result, a year later we find him fit and going strong, back in his old routine of digging, weeding and tending his large garden. The doctors have pronounced him100 percent healed. This serves as a reminder for us to focus on keeping active to strengthen our bones.

MOST YOUTH HAVE NO FEAR OF HEIGHTS

I heard young people in the back yard yelling, "Come on, Chip!" I reached the door just in time to see my son dive from the peak of our garage into the swimming pool—ten feet away. It was too late to stop him, but quick enough for my heart to stop momentarily. Though his friends were cheering him on, my fears ran rampant as I pictured him falling and being crushed beside the pool.

He told me later, "Don't worry Mom—I've been to Possum Kingdom where I dove into the lake from seventy foot cliffs." Gasp! I'm thankful that thirty years later, his common sense has kicked in and he no longer takes dares to dive from great heights.

This same lack of fear was evident in his uncle Don, who served as the ship's commander in a war zone during World War II. He dove off the mast of a ship into the ocean, proving one could escape a burning ship. Now that he's old, he's cautious about climbing up on a chair to change a light bulb.

Some of us were fearful of heights even when we were young. I climbed a windmill when I was ten years old. When approximately two-thirds of the way to the top, I looked down and became terrified at the thought of falling. When I looked up, the clouds were blowing over and it appeared the windmill was falling on top of me. I white-knuckled my grip and froze. I screamed for my brother to help me. He yelled back, "Just look straight ahead and climb down, one step at a time." That's still good advice. In life, it's wise to keep looking straight ahead and move in the right direction, one step at a time—until we reach a safe place.

Have You Fallen Lately?

I filled out a questionnaire at the doctor's office and they asked if I'd fallen more than once during the past year. *Nosey,* I'd fallen twice! One of the times I stumbled over a small rock in my son's yard; the other, I missed a six-inch step down from a curb. Does six inches strike you as a height to be fearful of? Regardless of how high I climb, I don't want to slip. When this old body falls, it makes one big splat.

My brother-in-law, Jim, jumped from a lower rung of a ladder and crushed his heel. The doctor told him, "Anyone over seventy has no business on a ladder." It's frustrating that once we get older, we don't dare climb any height because there's a danger of falling and getting hurt.

Though we shouldn't climb physically—spiritually, God isn't satisfied for us to stay on the bottom rung of the ladder. "I'm not afraid when you walk at my side" (Psa. 23:4 MSG). We thank God—He's present to keep us moving upward. He's our security, to lead us on—regardless of the altitude. Though we're earthborn, He doesn't intend for us to remain earthbound.

§

A short while back, I went to visit my sister-in-law Nan. When I arrived, I knocked on the door and heard a muffled plea, "Come help me!" I found her lying on the floor. She'd fallen and couldn't get up. With a few prayers and her cooperation, we were able to get her into a chair. Though there was no height involved, her age and weakness caused her to be unstable and she toppled while simply walking across the room. She expressed her gratitude, "I don't know what I would have done if you hadn't come." "Do not gloat over me, my enemy! Though I have fallen, I will rise" (Micah 7:8 NIV).

Sometimes we trip on the stairway to heaven, but God only counts it as failure if we refuse to try to get up. If God calls us to a task, we dare not allow fear to hamper our progress in climbing up to heaven. We're commissioned to keep moving upward. Our journey is not an escalator. It doesn't permit us to stand still while we're effortlessly lifted to the top.

Pride

Something we should fear more than physical heights is that of being snooty and high-minded with pride. Pride is an issue God insists we deal with at any age—but particularly as we grow nearer the end. It's then when we discover we have less ability to do things we once did. That hurts our pride.

Satan takes advantage of our weakened bodies and harasses us with his mocking, but this is an opportunity for pride to be lambasted. It forces us to be humble when we have to ask for help. Humility can grow stronger when we must seek assistance—again and again. God welcomes us to depend more on Him as well as those who are stronger than we are.

The older we get, the more we need to hold on to God as we recognize our limitations. Though we are weaker, we can link with the Father and accomplish great things. "God chose things the world considers foolish in order to shame those who think they are wise. And he chose things that are powerless to shame those who are powerful" (1 Cor. 1:27 NLT). Look at King David, the youngest and smallest of his family. He learned to depend on God in many different situations. God chose Gideon who, because of his inadequacies, argued with God about his assignment. If God chooses weak things, why wouldn't He choose older people—those who are weaker—to accomplish great things for Him?

§

Many years ago, the athletic world concluded that no man would ever break the four-minute mile barrier. A mental block made it seem impossible. An Englishman, Roger Bannister, burst the imaginary bubble in 1954. After Roger's breakthrough, an American named Steve Scott ran the sub-four-minute mile 186 times. Not only that, but an Irishman, Eanonn Goglin, was the first man over forty to shatter the four-minute mile myth. (Perhaps he could do that because he was over the hill, age-wise, and on a downhill slope!) Our minds often limit what we might actually be capable of doing.

DON'T ALLOW ANYTHING TO STOP GOD'S PURPOSE

A neighbor became incapacitated by several debilitating strains of arthritis. Ultimately, she was confined to her bed, scarcely able to move any part of her body.

She had her husband rig up a phone with a head set so she could continue her ministry of counseling and mentoring people—all over the world. Even without the ability to walk or get out of bed, she continued to climb higher in serving God through serving others. She explained, "I can endure the pain as long as God can use me in helping others."

When she knew the end was near, she requested that her family build a simple pine box coffin. She asked to be carried by pall bearers she had nurtured and carried spiritually. She couldn't climb high here, but in death, I'm sure she ascended to the heights.

§

God reaches out to those who walk in obedience. The Lord, who is stronger and wiser than any and everything in the universe, surveys the earth and reaches down to pick up the fallen and rescues those who admit they can't carry on alone. He lifts them up to be seated beside Him as an honored guest. *Pick us up and dust us off, Lord. We dare not fear the heights while we're climbing up to You.*

I love the idea of being seated in heaven with Christ Jesus. "Since you have been raised to new life with Christ, set your sights on the realities of heaven, where Christ sits in the place of honor at God's right hand" (Col. 3:1-2 NLT). If we're seated with Christ, we should be able to look down and see things from His perspective. Every trial will be an opportunity to see a possibility for growth!

§

There are younger and stronger pilgrims following us. I have grandchildren who are spiritually light years ahead of where I was at their age. I get excited about passing the baton to the next generation. Though I may not be able to go where they go, I can at least partially support them. "Lord, let my money, prayers and encouragement be like water and sunlight, empowering them to go and grow." We cheer them on, hoping they'll climb higher and possibly bring about the world-wide revival we long for. "Don't let anyone think less of you because you are young. Be an example to all believers in what you say, in the way you live, in your love, your faith and your purity" (1 Tim. 4:12 NLT).

A LITTLE CHILD SHALL LEAD THEM

My granddaughter, Belle, was five. Since her folks live in the Gulf Coast area of Texas, they seldom see even tiny flecks of snow. One Thanksgiving, they went to their cabin in Colorado. Belle prayed for snow. They only had a light sprinkling of snow, so when they went back in the spring, she prayed, "Lord, send a lot of snow." As they neared the cabin, the snow drifts became higher and higher until their van became stuck and they had to hike a half mile through deep snow to get to the cabin." Belle rode on her dad's shoulders, almost in tears. "Daddy, I'm so sorry I prayed for too much snow." She apologized over and over.

On the next trip, she prayed for *some* snow. They arrived at the cabin and after a couple of days with no snow, Belle's father, Chip, comforted her. "Belle, I'm sorry, but it looks as if your prayer won't get answered this time."

"Don't worry, Daddy, God is probably answering someone else's prayer." No wonder we're to become like little children. She looked higher than her own desires for answered prayers—to what others might be praying. Interestingly, that afternoon and evening they were blessed with a beautiful blanket of snow. How delightful that sometimes the Lord of heaven and earth chooses a child rather than a college professor or a rocket scientist to teach us. "Climb high, little one, seek God's higher plane."

§

As a child, I used to lie on my back to watch the clouds and identify those that looked like animals and people. One year when our daughter, Kathy, was three, she sat in my lap while we were traveling. (Before seat belts). She looked out the window and pointed, "I think I see Jesus."

Curious, I asked, "What does He look like?"

She paused before she answered, "I think He looks like my daddy."

Wouldn't it be wonderful if people looked at us as we grow older and were reminded of Jesus? Let your imaginations run wild—like that of a child and look to the heavens in anticipation of catching a glimpse of the magnificence of God.

Think of a small child reaching up and saying, "Hold you?" Who could resist that tender request? Somehow, I believe God is pleased when we reach up to say, "Hold you?" I'm so thankful we're assured that as we draw near to our Father, He comes close to us.

How exciting to think of our Majestic God, riding through the heavens on the clouds and waiting for us to reach out to Him. "He rides across the heavens to help you, across the skies in majestic splendor. The eternal God is your refuge, and his everlasting arms are under you" (Deut. 33:26-27 NLT). It's time for us to lose our fear of heights and fly high with God.

As we lift up Jesus, He becomes a magnet greater than the North Pole, drawing us to Him. The more we keep our eyes on Christ, the more we're drawn to Him. In turn, others will also be drawn because they see what He's done in our lives. People watch the way we live, the language we use and our attitudes in dealing with life.

§

I was honored when my twenty-three-year-old grandson asked if he could come spend some time with me and record our conversation. He not only wanted family stories, but my philosophy, my faith and what I'd learned in life. "Tell me about wisdom," he said. He asked about qualities to look for in a wife, where to place values and priorities. He recorded an hour and a half of our conversation. I could not have received a higher compliment than the confidence he placed in me. Perhaps we might record what we want our heirs to remember about our faith and philosophy. I wrote my testimony and a letter to each of my children and included those with my will. In doing so, I hope it inspires them to have high aspirations.

GO TO THE TOP OF THE MOUNT

Jesus led His chosen three to the Mount of Transfiguration and gave them a glimpse of the glory of God—how it will look when the resurrection takes us away in the clouds. Through scripture, we've been given a glimpse of this mountaintop experience that is able to sustain us during difficult days ahead.

I love an old song we sang when I was a child, "Lord, lift me up and let me stand—by faith on heaven's table land. A higher plane than I have found; Lord, plant my feet on higher ground." I don't want my feet to get bogged down in the cares of this world.

The apostle John had a vision of standing before an open door in heaven, with Jesus encouraging him to come up, so he could show him what was going to happen. Although we may not be given a vision of what will come in days ahead, I do believe God is opening a door for us to come higher. "After this I looked, and there before me was a door standing open in heaven. And the voice I had first heard speaking to me like a trumpet said, "Come up here, and I will show you what must take place after this." (Rev. 4:1-2 NIV). God welcomes us to keep on climbing.

STAY PREPARED

Scripture tells us we don't know the day or the hour when Jesus will return. Neither do any of us know when we'll be called home. One day Jesus will shout, "Ready or not, here I come." Now is the time of preparation. The door of the elevator is opening. As an elevator operator used to ask, "Going up?"

THINGS TO CONSIDER

1. Have you fallen in recent years? If so, what happened?

2. Are you becoming more cautious as you have more difficulty getting around?

3. Do you spend too much time thinking of the past and future and ignoring the present?

4. Are you hesitant to do things that seem a little more difficult than what you've been doing?

5. Are you limited by what you believe you can do?

6. Have disabilities that come with age affected your confidence and pride?

7. Are you looking for ways you can reach out to others even now?

8. Do you ask God to help you look at things from His perspective?

9. Are you willing to graciously accept help when you need it?

10. What are you doing now in preparation for eternity?

CHAPTER 15

I DON'T GET AROUND MUCH ANY MORE

"...dangers in the streets..." (Eccl. 12:5 NIV).

As people grow older, there's a tendency to 'roll up the sidewalks' at night and not venture far from home. With hearing and eyesight fading and a lack of balance, the possibility of getting injured increases. It's understandable why older people are more cautious about going out, especially at night.

With age, some withdraw socially or cut back on activities. Others have lost a spouse and explain they feel like a 'fifth wheel' with other couples. It's too much trouble to get dressed, or they're intimidated about going out alone. We must not morph into a recluse and smother opportunities for serving or intermingling with others.

Don't Shut out the World

A couple tragically lost their daughter in a car accident when the car she and her boyfriend were in crashed and burst into flames. They blamed him for saving himself and seemingly making no attempt to rescue her. In the depth of their sorrow, they pulled the shades in their home and lived like hermits, leaving the house only when absolutely necessary. That house became a tomb for the living dead—no more evidence of real life. Tragically, the giant spider of agoraphobia attempted to trap these parents inside his sticky web.

If you find yourself pulling back, let me encourage you to move out into the open sunlight and fresh air. "We throw open our doors to God and discover at the same moment that he has already thrown open his door to us. We find ourselves standing where we always hoped we might stand—out in the wide open spaces of God's grace and glory" (Rom. 5:1 MSG). God invites us to get out and discover a meaningful and fulfilling life.

When people pull away from others, they have a tendency to concentrate only on themselves and their circumstances. Their world shrivels. They renege from contributing to a world they were once committed to. Selfishness and self-pity move into the spare bedroom.

Some withdraw from others because there's been a conflict and they choose to withdraw rather than to work toward reconciliation. When I have a run-in with someone, there is a temptation to pull away, so he or she doesn't aggravate me further. When we're afraid we can't please others, we often avoid them, so they can't continue to walk all over us. Like Raggedy Ann dolls flopping around, we topple in any direction we're pushed. I'm making an effort to get beyond this problem. God made us with backbones.

Don't Put Selfish Interest above Others

In one of their weaker moments, my friends allowed her mother to make them promise they'd never place her in a nursing home. The mother now lives with them and is almost helpless. She consumes much of their time with her increasing demands. "Lord, help us never insist that others forfeit their own lives in order to pamper our petty whims." I was only half joking when I told my son, "If I ever get that demanding, take me out in the forest and tie me to a tree. You can tell me you'll come get me when I decide to be more considerate."

Still other older people are so stubbornly independent they might say, "Geppetto, go back to your bench. You ain't putting no strings on me!" These people get labeled as hard headed and uncooperative. You get the idea they only want to be around you if they can be in control of everything.

Strong-willed people have difficulty admitting they're wrong. They don't appear to listen to your opinion because they're thinking of a rebuttal. When some people get old, they become more domineering and manipulative. Deep down they may be cowards, but they crank up the volume of their voices in an attempt to bluff others into silence. Be careful, stubborn and strong-willed people may find they're left to be alone and become frustrated because people don't come around anymore. We cause people to distance themselves when we're set on getting our own way.

Fear on the Streets

When I taught in a maximum security prison, inmates sometimes asked, "Aren't you afraid of coming in here to teach?"

"I'm probably as safe here as I would be on the streets of near-by Houston." They nodded in agreement. I admit it was sobering when I had to sign a release that stated, "If you are ever taken hostage, there will be no deals or ransoms."

The prison was filled with con artists and possibly if there'd been a prison break, some inmates might have turned on me. But I believed sincerely there were those who would have died for me. I went there day after day, refusing to become a prisoner of fear. "The fear of man brings a snare, but whoever leans on, trusts in, and puts his confidence in the Lord is safe and set on high" (Prov. 29:25 AMP).

Other Dangers in the Streets

While attending a group in a nearby church, I met a woman who had been living on the streets of Houston for seven years, addicted to crack cocaine. She slept in a tent, buying and selling drugs. Her hard life was reflected in her appearance. She had a couple of front teeth missing and a glass eye. I never questioned her about these.

Growing weary of her lifestyle, the woman developed a burning desire to be set free in order to build a better life. She came to this church and they agreed to help her start over again. They found her temporary housing.

She had three typewritten pages of rehab centers to contact as possible places to go for help. She began calling, but had to scratch them off one by one, as each refused to accept her because she'd been drug-free for six months. Her hand shook while dialing the last number on the list. Thankfully, this Christian organization welcomed her and they have a reputation for great success with drug rehabilitation.

She was very relieved, because she felt that if she went back on the streets, she'd most likely be sucked back into a horrible lifestyle again. Now, I'm confident she'll come out of this eighteen month program with a powerful testimony. She'll be equipped to reach out and help change the lives of countless others who are trapped on the streets—just as she'd been.

Most of us have never experienced life on the streets, but the nightly news keeps us abreast of evils lurking outside. A police officer talked to a group of us and warned of predators stalking vulnerable women out on the streets—especially those of us who are older. We must be cautious, so we don't become a victim.

Some Precautions We Might Take:

1. Walk out of a store and stay in plain sight in the middle of parking lanes until you reach your car.

2. Don't park beside an enclosed van.

3. Be aware of schemes and scams that ask for your social security or credit card number.

4. Report the loss of your credit card immediately.

5. If you're coming out of a store at night, find someone else to walk beside you or ask a security guard to watch you until you get to your car.

6. Keep the doors of your car and your home locked, even in daytime.

7. Wasp spray is a better deterrent than mace.

8. Be observant of anyone that appears to be following or watching you.

9. Keep your cell phone where it is easily accessed. It is good to have one or two numbers you can speed-dial on your phone.

10. Never turn your back when your purse is in your shopping cart.

§

I was attending a seminar late one evening and had to park a distance from the auditorium. A young man on a bicycle slowly approached me from behind. As he peddled across from the other side of the street, he began to ease up closer, I got the feeling he was sneaking up to snatch my purse. There were people who were walking a distance ahead and I called loudly, "Wait for me!" When they turned to look back, the young man sped off on his bicycle.

§

A number of us came from an era when a handshake was as binding as a legal contract. We never locked doors to our homes and we left keys in our cars. Now, it's sad to find we're particularly vulnerable, because we assume others are honest and can be trusted. Crime has become rampant. As seniors, we're prime targets for scams, con artists and scheming predators with glib tongues. There are those who stand on street corners, claiming to be missionaries or poor hungry people begging for money or food. We learn through costly lessons to be wary of those we'd like to be able to trust. We've had to learn to guard information that might lead to identity theft.

Countless conniving and heartless people sneak into our homes via television, telephones and the internet. Tempting offers show up in our mailboxes, appearing to be from people who are seemingly legitimate and interested in our wellbeing. Their appeals get our attention as they promise money and perks or they prey on our compassionate hearts by urging us to donate to 'wonderful' charities. Legitimate skepticism has become a necessity. There is a need for a healthy fear out on the streets.

Solicitors may pretend to represent law officials, the military or other worthy causes. Experience has led me to make it a practice to only donate to those I *know* represent the charity they claim, as well as finding out how much of my donation goes to pay administrators. I particularly favor donating to friends and acquaintances that raise their own support and are under the umbrella of a legitimate ministry.

Fear of Going Forward

One night I had a dream where I was standing, facing a dark cave. The Lord stood in front of the entry. "Will you follow me?"

"Yes," I answered confidently.

"Will you follow me when you can't hear me?"

My answer was more guarded. "Yeess, Lord."

The third time He spoke, "Will you follow me when you can't see me?"

I swallowed hard, "I hope so, Lord. Help my unbelief." Soon after this dream, there was a time of testing with sickness, deaths, trauma and financial struggles. And yes, there were times when I could neither see nor hear the Lord and it became difficult to believe He was in the midst of these trials. I'm sure I wavered in the process, but God faithfully led me through some of the darker places in my life.

Don't be Afraid to Go Alone

A few days before my husband Carey died; a friend who led trips to Israel called him. Carey asked him to take me with him a couple of months later on a prearranged trip. About six weeks before our departure date, I fell and broke my ankle by tumbling down an incline in front of a grocery store. It had no warning or a railing to call my attention to the slope. I went back to the store a few days later with my cast on and found the manager. I suggested they put some kind of a warning on the edge of the ramp. He cringed. "We just talked about that in a meeting last week. We'll pay for whatever you've been out."

"That won't be necessary. I have insurance and I have no intention of suing."

"Wait! That's the reason we carry insurance. I'll send an adjuster to your home."

The adjuster came with his papers and got all the information he needed. A few weeks later, I had a call from the insurance company. They asked if I could come downtown to pick up the check. When I arrived, they handed me an envelope and I thanked them.

"Aren't you going to open it?"

"Oh, sure." I ripped the envelope open and was astonished when I saw the amount. "This is far more than my expenses. Didn't you make a mistake?"

"No, we can never remember anyone who tried to talk us out of giving them money. You've been most gracious. Go buy yourself some new clothes for the trip."

I'd been out of my cast only a few days before it was time to leave for Israel, so I moved cautiously. While in Israel, the group decided to go through Hezekiah's famous tunnel, which was dug 700 years before Christ, to bring water into the city of Jerusalem. Water still runs inside the tunnel over stones and uneven ground. Some questioned my decision to go with them, but one member of the tour group offered to walk with me and hold me steady. It's always comforting to have someone to lean on when we're going through rough places in life.

Jesus is always there for us to depend on but it's good to have flesh and blood to support us when we might possibly flounder and fall. We, too, need to remember to reach out to those we can help.

§

It's time to pay close attention to God's admonition: "See if there is any offensive way in me, and lead me in the way everlasting" (Psa. 139:24 NIV). On our way to walk on streets of gold, we ask God to remove any stones or hindrances that might cause us to stumble on our way. Listen for God's marching orders and prepare the way for others. "Walk out of the gates. Get going! Get the road ready for the people. Build the highway. Get at it! Clear the debris, hoist high a flag, a signal to all peoples!" (Isa. 62:10-11 MSG) This should take care of any fear in the streets.

THINGS TO CONSIDER

1. Are you staying closer to home than you have in times past? If so, for what reason?

2. Do you invite other seniors to go out with you?

3. Are you so independent that you don't allow others to help when you need them?

4. Do you feel others should take care of you?

5. What precautions do you take outside your home?

6. How do you protect your identity, such as your social security number, driver's license and credit cards?

7. Are you willing to give your energies to help others who are physically weaker?

8. Do you spend too much time thinking only of yourself and your circumstances?

9. Do you pay attention when others suggest you curtail some of your activities?

10. Do you feel shame about your limitations?

CHAPTER **16**

WHITE HAIR TELLS A STORY

"…when the almond tree blossoms…" (Eccl. 12:5 NIV).

A n almond tree covered with white blossoms could be Solomon's way of describing the white hair on an aging person. White blossoms on an almond tree signify it will produce sweet almonds—while one with pink blossoms produces bitter almonds. My prayer is that our white hair will signify we are sweet 'nuts'.

Even in their early forties, some discover gray hair sprouting. This brings to mind the words of an old song by Eben E. Rexford, "Darling, we are growing old—silver threads among the gold." Some pluck the gray hair for a time before deciding they'd rather have gray hair than no hair at all. Let's hope white hair doesn't indicate all the color has drained from our lives.

DEALING WITH HAIR PROBLEMS

At the right time, an almond tree loses its blossoms. Some people lose their hair because of a genetic disposition— others lose it because of medication. When my husband, Carey, had cancer and underwent chemo, his hair came out by the handfuls. He stood in front of the mirror one morning and grinned, "Since God knows the number of hairs on our head; it must take an angel full time to keep up with mine. He just had to subtract at least another hundred." He stared at his brush and shook his head, "I used to have a crew cut and now the crew is bailing out." He added, "I suppose it's just a matter of hair today, gone tomorrow."

People often try to hide their gray hair by putting color on it. Not many appreciate the words of Solomon when he explained that the gray hair of wisdom was more beautiful than the strength of young people. Of course, there are those who keep their natural gray color and may even playfully tease their children, "I earned every one of these gray hairs and you did your part in egging them on."

Lessons from Fruit-Bearing Trees

The almond tree is neither large nor impressive, but it has always been considered a valuable crop. In Old Testament times, almonds were symbolic of watchfulness and promise. Wouldn't it be fine if, as we grow older, we became more watchful of our thoughts and actions? What a wonderful witness this would be as one blossoms with the oncoming of age.

A blossoming fruit tree is a promise that wonderful fruit is on its way. In this season of life, we may bear different fruit than we produced in earlier years, but it is none the less significant.

Thankfully, the Master Gardener commissioned us to continue to bear fruit. He waters, prunes and cares for us in order to make us more productive. "You didn't choose me. I chose you.

I appointed you to go and produce lasting fruit " (John 15:16 CEV). I love to think of God calling to us and saying, "I choose you to bear beautiful fruit."

A Gnarled Old Pear Tree

In her early forties, my mother-in-law was left almost penniless with five children. When she was widowed, she had a baby only a few weeks old. With her husband's insurance money, she bought a very small, two bedroom, cracker-box style home for her family. Beside its tiny porch there was a gnarled old pear tree. It was ugly because it had broken limbs and a twisted shape. She wanted to cut the eyesore down, but no one offered to remove it for free and she had no money to pay someone to do the job. The first year it bore a few pears, so the next year she watered and fertilized it and was pleasantly surprised when the old tree yielded a bumper crop.

With each successive year, it appeared unlikely that it could survive another season, yet amazingly, it continued to bear fruit. She made hundreds of jars of pear preserves and created a recipe for a pear relish that many almost fought to get. These jars became standard gifts for friends and family for the remaining fifty years she lived in that home.

§

We, too, may look like the dickens, but we can continue to bear good fruit. Just because our skin may look like a wrinkled old prune or raisin, we refuse to believe that a prune is the fruit of the Spirit for older people. I like to think of it as evidence of condensed sweetness.

We're challenged to root ourselves deeply in Jesus in order to produce the fruit of the Spirit—love, peace, joy, patience, kindness, goodness, faithfulness, gentleness and self-control. We also need the courage to remove any roots of bitterness that feed angry attitudes which produce bad fruit. When Christ dwells in our heart, we send deep roots into His love. When God grafts us into His true Vine, we draw strength from being planted in Him and bear tasty fruit, regardless of our age. Jesus is that true Vine— we are His branches of fruitfulness.

§

Poochy stomachs and wrinkles don't disqualify us from becoming more beautiful inside than any model or Miss America. God puts us on stage as His model children at all ages. "I will still be the same when you are old and gray, and I will take care of you. I created you. I will carry you and always keep you safe" (Isa. 46:4 CEV).

It takes careful and severe pruning for a grapevine to bear its best fruit. As we yield to God and allow His Holy Spirit to prune off pride, anger and bad attitudes during the trying experiences we go through, we grow and produce a beautiful harvest. In the process, we stay connected to the Vine. We know that if we attempt to survive alone, we'll be like a severed branch, lying as a dead stick on the ground. A lifeless branch will never sprout or grow into a tree.

There are fruit- bearing seeds inside us that can perpetuate a legacy of good fruit for future generations. Seeds of God's Word sown in the lives of others have the potential of producing good crops for years to come.

JOHNNY APPLESEED

Johnny Appleseed, that is, John Chapman, dreamed of a country of blossoming apple trees where no one would ever need to go hungry. He spent the bulk of his adult life walking through New England, planting apple trees along the way. Tradition says he slept on the ground and often went barefoot. Some claim he wore a cooking pot on his head that he used to cook his meals. After 200 years, seeds coming from subsequent trees are still bearing fruit.

Johnny Appleseed envisioned planting trees to grow apples, but I believe he also understood the concept of producing spiritual fruit. He said his favorite book was the Bible. His actions reflected the Word of God and no doubt motivated him to also sow seeds of Truth along the way.

We're commissioned to scatter seeds of the gospel, so no one ever needs to go spiritually hungry. Nothing is sweeter than the fruit of the Spirit. "And those who are peacemakers will plant seeds of peace and reap a harvest of righteousness" (Jas. 3:18 NLT). As a peacemaker, we have the potential of leading others to the saving grace of Jesus. There's good soil all over the world where seeds of the gospel can be planted to grow and bear fruit.

§

The soil must be tilled to keep it from becoming hard and packed. Plowed ground holds the moisture and allows the sun and air to get to the seeds, which causes them to sprout and grow. "Sow for yourselves righteousness, reap the fruit of unfailing love, and break up your unplowed ground; for it is time to seek the

Lord, until he comes and showers righteousness on you" (Hos. 10:12 NIV). Lord, cultivate our hearts and keep them softened in order to continue to be fruitful.

EATING THE WRONG FRUIT

In the Garden of Eden, Eve was drawn to the one thing forbidden by God—the tree of the knowledge of good and evil. She and Adam were tempted because the fruit looked good and the devil assured them they would not die if they ate it. Satan dangled a hook in front of them with the temptation to know good and evil. Who doesn't want to be smart? This sounded reasonable. It was absolutely wrong, however, because God labeled it as forbidden fruit.

Adam and Eve fell for the devil's trap. Eating that fruit *did* open their eyes, but it also gave them a determination not only to *know* right, but to *be right*. This curse passed from one generation to the next. It's still with us today. This divisive arrogance is behind many arguments when our stubborn will determines to be right even at the expense of a good relationship with others.

Within itself, wisdom is good. When Solomon became king, God asked him what he wanted, and the king asked for wisdom. God was so pleased with his request that He not only gave him incredible wisdom but wealth and power as well.

True wisdom comes from God. It doesn't come from degrees or books. James, the brother of Jesus, tells us God is generous in giving wisdom to those who ask Him. He never considers an honest question to be dumb or stupid. Ignorance only shows up if we refuse to accept His wisdom or argue with His answer.

When we hear from God and we have a different opinion, we make the decision as to whether to do it our way or His way. God is not one to compromise. We waver like a wave of the sea when we try to decide what we'll do by tossing options about and becoming confused. This may ultimately cause us to make bad choices.

Hopefully, we've gained wisdom over the years that has proven to be of value. It would be pathetic if we've not learned some worthwhile things along the way. "Is not wisdom found among the aged? Does not long life bring understanding?" (Job 12:12 NIV). But be careful—there's a tendency as we grow older to insist we're always right.

WONDERFUL TREES

There is a description of the Tree of Life in Revelation. It is pictured as growing on each side of the River of Life, bearing new crops every month of the year. Its green leaves are to be used as medicine to heal the nations. We long for a time when there will be healing among the nations. What a marvelous prescription! It's free, cures every disease and has no list of adverse side effects written in small print.

We can make it a point to scatter words of encouragement to bring physical, emotional and spiritual healing to those around us. "Even in old age they will still produce fruit and they will remain vital and green" (Psa. 92:14 NLT). Even an old tree can offer a cool shade in the heat of summer.

At the retreat center, we had a huge oak tree near the gate that opened its arms to welcome and comfort every guest who came. I prayed for this old tree when hurricanes headed in from

171

the Gulf and encouraged it, "Hang in there old fellow, dig in your roots. Don't let the winds or storms topple you."

We, too, can lift our arms and offer comfort to those who are going through the storms of life. We become like trees planted beside a river whose roots go deep. The winds will not uproot us and long months of drought will not cause us to wilt. We continue to bear fruit because we've tapped into the Water of Life.

What a beautiful plan God has for us. "Even to your old age and gray hairs I am he, I am he who will sustain you. I have made you and I will carry you; I will sustain you and I will rescue you" (Isa. 46:4 NIV). Mamaw kept her old pear tree around because it continued to be fruit-bearing. I believe God is happy to sustain us so we can continue to bear good fruit.

It is my desire that the older I grow and the whiter my hair, the more people will feel free to come to me for comfort. God has offered His comfort to me on many occasions. He fills me until some of that comfort overflows into the lives of others. I'd love for the leaves growing on the branches of my life to offer healing for the emotional hurts and pain of those who need to be healed.

THINGS TO CONSIDER

1. How do you deal with a body that is growing older?

2. How might you continue to grow and bear good fruit?

3. Are there roots of anger or bitterness in your life that need to be rooted out?

4. Are you sending deeper roots into the Word of God to tap into His wisdom and truth?

5. Are you scattering seed in the lives of younger people so they will continue to bear fruit long after you are gone?

6. Do you offer your arms of comfort to those who are hurting?

7. Are you more interested in looking good or being good?

8. In what areas have you been pruned by God?

9. Do you ever risk spoiling a good relationship because you are determined to be right?

10. How can God use you in healing the hurts of others?

CHAPTER 17

WHERE HAS ALL MY ENERGY GONE?

"...the grasshopper drags himself along..." (Eccl. 12:5 NIV).

Autumn is a time when it appears nature is slowing down to take a long, deep breath. The trees relax and drop leaves like giant brown snowflakes, floating down to snuggle close to the ground. Ah! Breathe deeply and allow the cares of the world to slide from your shoulders.

However, the fall season of life has a way of siphoning strength and energy from our bodies. We experience our own energy crisis. It starts in the feet and legs and works its way up. I find myself huffing and puffing after going up one flight of stairs. As we grow older and move more slowly, we're thankful that God will never run off and leave us behind.

§

We can regain, or at least stall, some waning physical energy by purposely becoming more active. It's encouraging to learn many muscles can be rebuilt at any age. Jack La Lane, an exercise guru, continued his exercise routine well into his nineties. Scripture tells us that exercise and workouts are good, but keeping fit as a Christian prepares us to be strong spiritually.

There are YMCA's and senior exercise programs in many communities. In our subdivision, we have an eighty-three-year-old woman who leads water aerobics—which is particularly enjoyable for me. Psychologists suggest that exercise not only elevates our energy level and general well-being, but it also strengthens us emotionally, by lifting our spirits. In spite of all our efforts to keep this old physical body strong, someday it will grow weary.

§

More guests were on their way to my house after a stream of visitors. I needed more groceries. I realized how much my energy level lagged when I got out of the car to go into the grocery store. I was dragging along, pushing a cart and rehearsing how tired I felt. When I realized where my thoughts were taking me, I threw back my shoulders and began to repeat, "The joy of the Lord is my strength." I quickened my step and deliberately smiled and spoke cheerfully to a woman heading out of the store with her stash of groceries. Almost immediately, a portion of my strength returned and I reaped the benefits of the Lord's joyous strength.

Tiredness versus Weariness

Tiredness and weariness aren't in the same category. Hard work may wear us down physically, but we can feel revitalized after a good night's sleep. I call that a *good tired*. Weariness affects us emotionally and seeps deeply into our bones, settling in through the long hours of the night. The following morning we still don't feel rested or energized.

When we're emotionally dragging, our faces usually reflect tell-tell signs of despondency. Discouragement is sculpted on long faces. Our shoulders droop and the sparkle in our eyes is displaced by dull lifelessness, announcing to the world that we're frazzled in mind and body.

Moods can be detected by our tone of voice. Depression is evident in the first word my friend speaks when answering the phone. You know her emotions are bottoming out when she responds with a slow and mournful, "Hel—lo." A weary heart is evident in a gloomy outlook.

Don't Drag Around!

The word 'drag' could form a negative acronym to remind us to refuse to be like an old grasshopper dragging himself around.

D – droopy

R – resigned

A – apathetic

G – grumpy

Our bodies may be weary and weak, but our spirits can keep on hopping, and who knows, some of that energy may spill over into the physical realm. By God's grace, He can keep us moving forward.

I'm confident we can reverse the curse of looking and sounding weary, and a good place to start is with our tone of voice. When we determine to sound upbeat, our bodies follow suit and our shoulders begin to lift. Try an experiment. Say something cheery while maintaining a sour expression on your face. It's not easy.

As the muscles in our faces relax, our lips curl up instead of sagging and it often motivates others to smile. Even a tiny baby frequently smiles when others smile at him. Smiling is contagious. Let a smile be the trigger that releases a bullet that explodes with joy when it strikes those around us. A smile on your face is a reflection of a cheerful heart.

Count Your Blessings

Possibly one way to help change a dreary day is to sit down and make a list of blessings, thanking God for each of them. In a list of things we're grateful for, include things that seem all wrong. Though it's difficult to look at bad things in a positive way, it is in direct obedience to Scripture. We're told to rejoice when we run into trials and problems, because they help us develop endurance and strength of character. Frankly, if I had a vote, I'd vote for another way to build character, but I don't find God giving other options.

It's often difficult to remain upbeat because the world has conditioned us to emphasize pessimism. People grumble and complain about the weather, the traffic, neighbors, their families and the economy. Pay attention to the conversations you engage in. Does your input add to negative comments or do you offer delightful input?

It's time to appoint ourselves as a committee of one to spread hope and joy. It not only helps others feel better, but it begins to drip off our chins and waters our own souls. When our personalities sparkle, we can be a magnet, drawing others out of their despondency.

A CHALLENGE TO PRAISE

Praise challenges us to come into the glorious presence of God, our Abba Father. As I lift my voice to praise Him, I join the apostle Paul in his declaration, "I have learned by now to be quite content whatever my circumstances. I'm just as happy with little as with much.. . . I've found the recipe for being happy whether full or hungry, hands full or hands empty. Whatever I have, wherever I am, I can make it through anything in the One who makes me who I am" (Phil. 4:12-13 MSG). Even as our physical strength declines, our inner spiritual strength can continue to grow.

I'M NOT AS STRONG AS I ONCE WAS

Our loads are often more difficult to carry because of age, but they become so much lighter when we rehearse the truths of God's promises. Try an experiment. Find uplifting scriptures to cover your bathroom mirror. Read them regularly. Better still, memorize some of them or at least write them on three by five cards to carry with you to read aloud when you have bits of time; while waiting for the light to change or waiting for a prescription to be filled. You'll be surprised at how much better you feel and how much your energy is restored.

HANG ON TO YOUR PATIENCE

I visited my sister-in-law at an assisted living facility. The next morning, we noted a resident seated at a nearby table fussing and fuming because he didn't get his meal as quickly as some others. I was curious as to what he had on his agenda for the day that made him so impatient about getting his breakfast. I noticed him later in the lobby, sitting and staring into space as if he were simply waiting for the next meal. I suspect he has a habit of being impatient, demanding to get what he wants—when he wants it.

A long-suffering, godly woman lived in a foreign country that persecutes Christians. She was thrown into prison because of her faith. In a tiny cell in solitary confinement, she was starved, beaten and interrogated. She patiently endured. She said her only regret was that she had not memorized more Scripture to recite. She thought of ways to reach out to others by sharing her meager rations with men in nearby cells. She pulled elastic from her clothing so she could shoot scraps of food to other prisoners. As she slung a small piece of bread down the corridor, she sang, *Amazing Grace*. She prayed and the Lord gave her the patience to survive until she was released—months later. "You won't see us drooping our heads or dragging our feet! Cramped conditions here don't get us down" (2 Cor. 5:6 MSG). Life handed her a splintered tool to work with, but she still planted a beautiful garden—even in prison.

"Don't worry about anything; instead, pray about everything. Tell God what you need, and thank him for what he has done. Then you will experience God's peace, which exceeds everything we can understand. His peace will guard your hearts and minds as you live in Christ Jesus" (Phil. 4:6-7 NLT). The most difficult trials often reveal either our greatest strength or our greatest weakness. Pay attention to what emotions come up when a situation turns sour.

I'll have to admit, it's hard to stay patient when the road is longer and harder than we anticipated. I've found it helpful to do good things for others. Some days I start off tired, not in the mood to do much of anything. I have to get behind myself and push to get jump-started. Sure enough, if I do something for someone, I usually uncover a fresh battery of strength and get recharged.

When our children were small we knew of a family that struggled financially. One night we bought bags of groceries to take to their home and put them on their front porch. Our children rang the door bell and scurried into the bushes to hide. We watched from a distance as the family opened the door and looked to see if they could find who'd blessed them. It gave us a shot of adrenalin and we chuckled every time we thought about what we'd done. It is energizing to help others.

§

If anyone ever had a reason to be weary, God does. Can't you see Him looking down on the dismal way His children have blown it through lack of respect, sin and selfishness? It's difficult to understand how, after centuries of dealing with unfaithful children, He restrains Himself from hurling all of us into outer darkness. "Don't you know? Haven't you heard? The Lord is the eternal God, Creator of the earth. He never gets weary or tired. His wisdom cannot be measured. The Lord gives strength to those who are weary" (Isa. 40:28-29 CEV).

He infuses us with His strength to steady worn-out knees and to lift our spirits. We'll speak to our bodies and tell them to get up and get on with life. I don't understand why God is so patient in reaching out to us—but I'm forever grateful. "I've been carrying you on my back from the day you were born, and I'll keep on carrying you when you're old. I'll be there, bearing you when you're old and gray" (Isa. 46:3 MSG). Just as we bless others with a cup of cool water, God blesses us by refreshing us, energizing every cell in our bodies. We dare not wander far from God, because He is our strength.

"Are you tired? Worn out? Burned out on religion? Come to me. Get away with me and you'll recover your life. I'll show you how to take a real rest. Walk with me and work with me—watch how I do it. Learn the unforced rhythms of grace. I won't lay anything heavy or ill-fitting on you. Keep company with me and you'll learn to live freely and lightly" (Matt. 11:29 MSG).

As we grow older and move slower, we can be thankful that our Lord adjusts His pace to stay close to us. He orchestrates simple rhythms of grace and invites us to dance. Like an old tree in the wind, I creak a bit when I sway, but I'm pleased to see Him smiling His approval as He stands nearby and watches me.

THINGS TO CONSIDER

1. Do you get discouraged because you have less energy than you once did?

2. Do you have an exercise program to help you stay energized?

3. If you are depressed or weary, can you think of things you might do to recover?

4. Does your tone of voice sound upbeat?

5. What do your conversations focus on?

6. Make a list of your blessings.

7. Do you consciously try to be cheerful and kind?

8. Have you learned to be content in every situation you find yourself in?

9. Would it help if you knew others were cheering you on your journey?

10. Have you reached out to help someone recently?

CHAPTER 18

HAVE YOUR DESIRES FADED?

"...desire is no longer stirred" (Eccl. 12:5 NIV).

Some look at this *desire* Solomon speaks of as applying to sexuality. Though this is possibly the major aspect alluded to, there are other messages relating to age as we allow our dreams and goals to fade away.

Okay, fellow journeymen. We have a choice. We can succumb to burn out, rust out or admit we're just tired and worn out. You may hear those who are burned out say, "I've had it and I'm sick and tired of it all," or, "I give up." Those who rust out may sit down to rest and decide to stay put like the Tin Man in the Wizard of Oz who became immobilized by staying stuck so long he squeaked when forced to move. Come on, Holy Spirit, pour on Your oil to loosen us up. Your anointing beats WD-40 any time. "How wonderful, how beautiful when brothers and sisters get along! It's like costly oil flowing down head and beard" (Psa. 133:1 MSG). This description doesn't paint an appealing picture of oil dripping all over, but if it represents the anointing of God flowing down, I'm shouting, "Bring it on!"

Many of us may justifiably be worn out. This old body has run the rat race and is tired from trudging along. We wear out even doing the things we want to do because our bodies aren't functioning very well. But even then we can conclude, *We may be on our last leg, but that one stands solid on the Rock.* We migrate closer to God's inner circle to become like a plumb line as our lives and hearts line up with His Word.

KEEP HOPE ALIVE IN DIFFICULT TIMES

How can you dream or even have hope when it feels like you've been punched in the pit of your stomach? There have been times when I've needed God to help me catch my breath. One particular time, I was tempted to throw up my hands and quit when faced with what appeared to be an intolerable situation. I had to cling to God to keep from running from the problem, even while God whispered, "Hold steady."

Carey got involved with another woman because he allowed his desires to drift. The flattery and flirting of an older college student enticed him. When I found out about the affair, I almost cratered. The night I discovered his unfaithfulness, I sobbed, took a long, deep breath and repeated the marriage vows I had made—"for richer or poorer, for better or worse." This, I concluded, was a part of the 'worse.' In a strange way, repeating this commitment somehow knocked the teeth out of the enemy's attack and sucked a portion of the poison from my wounds.

Though there were times I considered leaving and ripping up my marriage license, deep within there was a burning desire to make it work, even if Carey didn't seem particularly interested.

I struggled back and forth. Probably the children were my main reason for not bailing out.

I knew unforgiveness was the number-one cause for divorce, so I made up my mind to approach it from that angle. The enemy kept whispering, "He doesn't deserve forgiveness." That seemed true, but it didn't negate my responsibility to ask God to help me learn to forgive. The hurt and pain took time to heal, but I kept clinging to my commitment. The children and I are so glad I did.

> He built a barrier to shut me out,
>
> With bricks of rejection, pain and doubt.
>
> But forgiveness and love sent out a call—
>
> He came back to tear down that wall.

Over twenty years later, on our thirty-fifth anniversary, Carey wrote me a letter, only six months before he died. It said all I had wanted him to say years before. He wrote that he believed God picked me for him. He mentioned things he'd done and failed to do that could have destroyed our marriage. Included in this list of compliments was gratitude for a forgiving spirit.

§

Some desires we once had may have grown dim in later years—or dreams have been abandoned, because our activities are more constricted. Hope that once rose over the horizon appears to be sinking with the sunset of life. It's time to vow to search for the hope of tomorrow. It is comforting to know that though everything in this life will wear out, rust out or needs to be thrown

185

out—we are restored, renewed and rewarded when we determine to complete whatever plans Almighty God has for us here.

WE CAN SHOW LOVE AT ANY AGE

Age isn't a factor in our ability to show love. During a seminar, it dawned on me—I'd inadvertently pulled back from friends and family because five loved ones died one after another—my father, my mother, my son, my brother-in-law and my brother. I still had a desire to show and receive love, but perhaps I surmised it wouldn't hurt as much to lose someone if I weren't so involved in that person's life. After the seminar, I went to my children and asked for forgiveness. "I'm sorry I pulled away from you. We all miss out when I'm not open and expressive of my love."

§

Love may be shown in different ways. My sister's mother-in-law could hardly make ends meet as an extremely poor widow. Not wanting to accept money from her children, she took in boarders and made and sold homemade loaves of bread. She supplemented her income further—by ironing. My sister paid her to iron her husband's starched white shirts. One day Sis apologized, "I'm so sorry you have to do all this ironing." Her mother-in-law turned slowly and smiled. "You don't know how much love I can iron into my son's shirts."

This is a wonderful time of life to enlarge our tents of love. Love can be a shelter, a place of comfort from the heat and pressures of daily living. We can stretch it wide as a protection from the storms of life. "Enlarge the place of your tent, stretch your tent curtains wide, do not hold back; lengthen your cords, strengthen your stakes" (Isa. 54:2 NIV).

§

When I taught in prison, some of the inmates told me I acted as if I really cared for them. I assured them I did. Then I asked if they had others who loved and cared for them. Several responded, "I don't think I ever had anyone who cared whether I lived or died." My heart ached. This should remind us to make it our mission to share love and encouragement with those we meet—even those whose actions don't appear to merit such love. Often those who deserve our love the least actually need it the most. We can reach out to them by phone, e-mails, letters or text messages. We may never know how much small gestures may touch and change lives.

EXPAND GOALS AND DESIRES

We can enlarge our dreams and goals for the future. Desire has been defined as a deep longing, a wish expressed in words. If we think of an idea long enough, we'll begin to talk about it—and speaking aloud empowers it. As we continue to mull over our dreams, we'll find ourselves being drawn toward those possibilities. God is ready to help us accomplish far more than anything we can do alone.

AN ASSIGNMENT

List various aspects of your life on paper under these headings: Physical, Emotional, Intellectual, Educational, Spiritual,

Relationships with Friends and Relationships with Family. Make columns underneath each category. Write under each area what you'd like to accomplish in the next three months. Don't make these plans too lofty, but slightly beyond what you're doing right now. Draw a line under these and then write, "Goals for the next year." Stretch yourself a little more. My first goal in writing was to publish a one-page article—which was all I could do at that time. I began to polish my writing skills by journaling each day.

Continue with projections for the following year, expanding each phase of your life. For the third year, dream still larger. The norm is to set short-term goals too high and long-term goals too low. The underlying directive is to commit the project to the Lord, knowing that He is the secret ingredient of success.

Pull this plan out of the files periodically and read it aloud. Remember: rehearsing what we want in life draws us in the direction of our dreams—sometimes with little conscious effort or planning. Ultimately, it's God's call. Our finite minds can make all kinds of elaborate plans, but God has the last word. Human tendency is to settle for what looks good. God holds out for what *is* good.

My sister-in-law, Mickey, is past ninety years old and just announced she's ready to begin writing again. She published two books over twenty years ago. Though a detached retina has caused her to be blind in one eye and she doesn't see clearly out of the other, she refuses to sit back and do nothing.

Her husband, Don, is ninety-five and still goes to work most days to the farm implement business he established just after World War II. He sold it to his son a number of years ago, but He continues to go to work there. He knows almost every farmer in his territory and does a lot of 'PR' for their operation.

Don also has a hobby of collecting antique implement seats from all over the world. He fulfills his desire to be active and do something he enjoys. As he adds to his collection, he finds pleasure in discovering a one-of-a-kind seat that may have been in someone's barn for a hundred years or more. Many of the seats come from foreign countries. He pulls a display of the seats to county fairs behind an antique tractor and explains their origins to those who are interested.

§

Our desires sometimes get tangled with expectations. One day Carey complained, "I hardly accomplished anything I planned today. Phone calls and people dropping by disrupted my day."

"Were you able to help them?"

"Well, yes. Everyone thanked me for my input."

"Perhaps God made your schedule for you today."

"Yeah," he laughed, "you're probably right."

God knows exactly where we are—whether with failing health and energy or perhaps we're simply discouraged. He never expects more of us than He's provided the strength for us to accomplish. Our capabilities may cause the heights of our ambitions to shrink but the trick is to learn to adjust.

GOD WHISPERS WORDS OF ENCOURAGEMENT

Ted* came to the retreat center, worn out and discouraged. He felt out of touch with God and wondered whether he could find his way back. He sat on the glider on the porch at the little Casa we built down in the woods. Suddenly, two sparrows flew directly in front of his face. This startled Ted, but reminded him, "What is the price of two sparrows—one copper coin. But not a single sparrow can fall to the ground without your Father knowing it" (Matt. 10:29 NLT). Ted surmised God still considered him to be of great value.

In the evening, Ted returned to the porch. Two deer wandered out of the forest to graze on the meadow in front of him. He remembered, "As a deer gets thirsty for streams of water, I truly am thirsty for you, O God" (Psa. 42:1 CEV). He then recognized his growing thirst for God. He grabbed his Bible and began to read—to drink in the Living Water of Life.

It had been some time since he'd read the Bible. Almost moment by moment, as he read, he felt himself revitalized. He was excited to be learning more about the rewards of following Jesus. He searched for God and found Him. This fulfilled his desire, his need to receive God's grace and mercy.

The next morning, Ted walked out on the hill toward a swing under a vine-covered arbor. I watched him running back toward the house. Breathlessly he pointed and said, "I looked up and watched a bald eagle sail over and light at the top of that tall walnut tree. God reminded me I can still run and not be weary. I can mount up as on wings of eagles. I'm so encouraged. God is fulfilling the desires of my heart. I know that now I can return home and face my problems with confidence."

REFOCUS

As we grow older, the desire for material things usually begin to fade. They fail to entice us as they did in younger years. "But

Christ has shown me that what I once thought was valuable is worthless" (Phil. 3:7 CEV).

I have a great desire to bring hope and encouragement to those who age. I'd like to think I could encourage every senior with the fact they can expect God to work in their lives until the very end.

When we line up our desires with the things God desires for us, we follow under the banner Jesus carries and walk in an atmosphere of victory day by day. "May he give you the desire of your heart and make all your plans succeed. We will shout for joy when you are victorious and will lift up our banners in the name of our God" (Psa. 20:4-5 NIV). We, like David the king, who had a desire to build a temple for the Lord, may need to pass some of our desires on to our children or grandchildren for them to fulfill. We hand the baton to them and encourage them to keep on running.

KEEP SHINING

The night Carey died, our daughter Kathy and I drove home from the hospital. A huge shooting star blazed across the sky. "Look!" she exclaimed. "Just like Dad, he too went out in a blaze of glory." This can be our greatest desire—to shine even brighter as we near the end.

THINGS TO CONSIDER

1. Have you given up on dreams that might still be revived?

2. Are you rusting out, burning out or just feel like you're wearing out?

3. What has been the most difficult thing in your life to get over?

4. Have you been able to forgive everyone involved—including yourself?

5. Are you committed to continue to walk in forgiveness?

6. Are you willing to follow the assignments in this chapter and set goals for different aspects of your life?

7. Do you continue to reach out in love to those around you?

8. Do you get upset when your plans get interrupted?

9. What would you like to set as your main focus in life now?

10. Do you look for ways that God is at work around you?

CHAPTER 19

CHECK-OUT TIME

"...man goes to his eternal home..." (Eccl. 12 5 NIV).

As mortals we're confined to live within the limits of time and space. By using the Hubble space telescope astronomers have concluded there are billions of other galaxies far beyond the Milky Way. If it's impossible to fathom an end to space, why should we be surprised that time is also unending? I accept both these unfathomable truths by faith. Faith is the confidence that our hope will someday burst forth in full-blown reality.

Man's inventions and accomplishments, within themselves, are mind-boggling. Since we accept these, why would we hesitate to believe that the Creator of.the universe is far more creative and wise than all man's knowledge combined? We stand in awe that He's powerful enough to create a kingdom that will last forever.

Our Father planned everything from the beginning. He arranged a pit stop for us here on earth before we move into the outer realm of eternity. The Father and His Son Jesus are setting up this kingdom for those who accept His invitation to come and live with Him forever as a part of His family. Isn't it breathtaking to know we've been invited to live under the canopy of heaven because we accepted His Son? In His goodness He's adopted us as His children.

Jesus became our perfect role model and completed His mission here on earth before God took Him back to heaven to prepare a mansion for us. There will be no mortgage or rent because the price for this eternal home is paid in full. Jesus took care of our sins in order to make us look good when we stand beside Him.

DIFFERENT FRUIT IN STAGES OF LIFE

Each stage of life provides an opportunity for growth. We have opportunities to develop the various fruits of the Spirit. At the birth of our children, we welcomed these helpless infants. How surprising when those tiny bits of humanity dominated our lives until we were exhausted. Their demands and cries seemed endless. This became a prime time to develop the fruit of longsuffering.

Their childhood is a time for them to grow and learn. This period lasts a little longer. Parents are stretched as they search for the wisdom to properly train and discipline their children. Before we had children, we may have had many theories and no children but then, we had many children and no theories. Children struggle to learn skills while the parents struggle to learn patience.

Adolescence is a fairly short period of time, though to parents it may seem unending. It is a time when many young people act cocky and invincible. Parents may have to practice greater self-control to keep from being frustrated and overwhelmed. Teens may dislike their parents and parents may be stretched to care very much for their teenagers. Come on self-control!

Adulthood spans many years of working and achieving. It's a time to wrestle with faithfulness; both with family and jobs. Challenges to remain faithful come from every direction. We make continuous decisions about our priorities in life. God calls us to be faithful.

This period may overlap middle age. Hopefully, empty nests allow us to reach out with kindness to include others outside our family. It calls for wisdom as we help our children evaluate their purpose in life and plan for the future. During this period of time things may get blurry because some refuse to admit they're growing older. You'll likely hear people grumble about their age until they reach the point of being able to brag about how old they are. Regardless, none of us can deny the need to learn kindness during this transition.

Moving over into the arena of aging, it becomes more obvious that our physical bodies don't function as well as they once did. But this is a time for love to mature. It embodies every other fruit of the Spirit. As various physical maladies bombard our bodies, the ability to show and express love is tested—but love ripens as we hold steady and prepare for eternity.

§

Eventually, Father Time cracks open the door to reveal the Grim Reaper lurking nearby. It will be God's timing when our lives are snuffed out and we're catapulted into eternity, a world without end. We need to take a deep breath now, because what we'll encounter will leave us breathless, staring in wonder at all God has prepared for us.

I think of a wedding ring, referred to as a pledge of eternal commitment. Jesus, as the bridegroom of the church, offers us His eternal commitment of love that will encircle us forever.

I've tried to grasp eternity in my hands, but realized my hands were surrounded by His. I peeked and saw He'd written my name in the palm of His hand. He holds me tight. All the demons of hell can never pry His hand open to rob, kill or destroy me now. "I give them eternal life, and they shall never perish; no one can snatch them out of my hand. My Father, who has given them to me, is greater than all; no one can snatch them out of my Father's hand. I and the Father are one" (Jn. 10:27-30 NIV).

When Does God Heal?

Our friends took in a foster baby with a tiny micro cephalic head. The doctors told them the infant was extremely mentally retarded and would never live a normal life, but the couple fell in love with the baby and made the decision to adopt her. With mountains of prayer and heaps of love, the child's head began to grow and she began to develop normally. Within a few short years, she was pronounced bright and forever changed—with no adverse defects. She was beautiful. We'll never know how much their love and prayers overruled the handicap, but I believe God blessed their efforts with an ongoing miracle.

My music teacher had a Down's Syndrome child. She believed unswervingly that with love, prayer and tireless effort she could help him overcome his disability. It was devastating to her when years later Billy showed little improvement. We don't always understand God's ways, but I'm confident Billy will be made whole in eternity. One great day, if He chooses, God may reveal why He heals some people here, while others must wait until eternity. We are assured that after a few short years on earth, we can live throughout eternity with Him—bright, beautiful and whole with no disabilities.

Some with severe problems teach us wondrous lessons. We must never be limited by our preconceived ideas of what will happen. Dean was born with Prader-Willi Syndrome. His parents were told the infant would not live. Day after day he survived. As he clung to a thread of life, they were told he would never walk or talk. His mother carried him until she could hardly lug him around.

After five years of consistent effort they taught Dean to walk, but he never learned to speak more than a few words. His parents worked with him over the years, but at age sixteen, when they could no longer handle him, they placed him in a special needs home. In that home, at age eighteen, he suffered heart failure and died.

At his funeral his three older brothers each stood up to tell of the lessons they learned from their develop-mentally handicapped brother, Dean. One remarked, "He taught me unconditional love because he would run and embrace me every time I walked in the door." The second said, "He taught me gratitude by jumping up and down and squealing when I brought him the smallest gift—even a stick of gum." The third brother choked up, "He taught me joy, as he laughed at a kitten, a bird or even a fly on the wall." Truly, this young man with little mental capacity taught great lessons; gifts even brilliant people rarely leave as a legacy. In a very unusual way he fulfilled the purpose God had for him on this earth.

His mother said the greatest miracle was his birth. It was then she said, "I turned to God for strength, wisdom and patience." Her example of faith and trust in God were a powerful influence that led many of her family members to Jesus.

§

A short time before my husband died, a man came up to him at church and told him, "I saw you in a vision totally well and healed." Carey thanked him for his encouraging words, but then asked, "Did you see me here or in heaven?" The man stammered, "I don't know." Carey's healing did not come until he passed from this life.

Inconveniences and pain arising in this late stage of our lives may be an incubator to cultivate and water the fruit of the Spirit that will last throughout eternity. If this is true, then we must regulate the thermostat so our tempers don't flare up or our hearts don't grow complacent and cold, thwarting our spirit in its development.

BE CONFIDENT THAT WE CAN MAKE IT TO THE OTHER SIDE

As a child we played a game called, 'Red Rover, Red Rover.' We stood in two lines facing each other, with hands clasped tightly. One side would call out to the other, "Red Rover, Red Rover, let (child's name) come over." The named child would run from the opposite side full force to try to break through the line. They picked what they considered to be the weakest link and hoped for a breakthrough. In a similar sort of way, Satan is forever looking for our weakest or most vulnerable spot in an attempt to break into our lives with negative thinking.

We stand with our arms linked with Jesus—ready for God to call our name. Jesus runs with us to make sure we successfully break through death into eternal life. We'll charge full speed ahead, because He opens the way.

I'm in the process of putting my visa aside from this world. The Lord completed my citizenship papers in heaven when He adopted me as His own. The Father confirms His approval as banners and shouts await our arrival. We've been learning to speak 'love' because that's the universal language of heaven.

Our Savior will someday equip us with spacesuits that will replace these earth suits. Unlike the bulky spacesuits of astronauts, our weightless spirits affirm we are indeed citizens of high heaven. We'll be prepared for the countdown!

No Turning Back

We sold the farm with its three houses, a barn and a storage shed packed with equipment. I almost came to reckless abandon in getting rid of things. Ultimately, I called Good Shepherd Mission and they brought three men, a large truck and a trailer and filled them with everything except essentials to take their resale shop.

Though a few things were taken inadvertently, I cannot tell you what a weight was lifted from my shoulders when I saw them drive out the gate with the accumulation of the past fifteen years. It will bring even greater relief when we leave behind all the excess baggage of this world.

When the time comes for us to lay it all down, I'd like to think we can leave as peacefully as the sunset laying it down for the night. I pray that we will approach death with the same perspective as William Cullen Bryant did in his poem, *Thanatopsis*. "We go with an unfaltering faith, to lie down to pleasant dreams."

While we still have an opportunity, we can be the voice of God's encouragement—proclaiming the good news to those who struggle in this world. We offer them a portion of God's tow rope to hold onto. This life line never grows slack, but is kept taut by hope that leads up to Him.

Time and the stages of this life pass quickly. Soon the conductor will cry out "All aboard." In one sense, it seems we just climbed on board, and now we discover we're almost there. We're been compared to fog or a wisp of smoke, quickly burned away or carried away by a puff of wind.

We're no longer so focused on growing older but on growing upward. We determine to face each day with the beauty of a sunrise— in great expectancy for the day. "...because of the tender mercy of our God, by which the rising sun will come to us from heaven to shine on those living in darkness and in the shadow of death, to guide our feet into the path of peace" (Lk. 1:78-79 NIV).

As the last gift of my going-away party is unwrapped, I'll put away my toys and haul the rest of my stuff to Goodwill, hoping it will brighten someone else's day. Whether it's a Rolex or a Timex, neither is needed any more. Even though some of our things are not worn out—we are.

I think I hear them singing, "Get on board little children, there's room for many a more." Won't you come along?

THINGS TO CONSIDER

1. Is it difficult for you to think outside the realms of time and space?

2. What has been the most difficult stage of your life?

3. Are you convinced that prayer and love are two of the most powerful forces in the universe?

4. How do you see that we are challenged to work on pride at this stage of life? Explain.

5. Do you still struggle with things you see happening in the world?

6. Do you believe God plans to perfect all things in eternity?

7. Do difficulties that show up in your life make you bitter or better?

8. Do you live your life in such a way that you would be content for God to call you home any time?

9. Do you have a tendency to question why God allows bad things to happen?

10. What lessons have you learned during each stage of your life?

CHAPTER 20

GRIEVING OUR LOSSES

"...and mourners go about the streets" (Eccl. 12:5 NIV).

Tears wash over the soul as a cleansing agent—a provision God gave us for grief. It plays its part in healing a broken heart. But God would not have us set up camp and live in a state of sadness. Jesus is ready and willing to seek us out, to come help us bear our burdens. "The Spirit of the Sovereign Lord is on me. . . . He has sent me to bind up the brokenhearted, to proclaim freedom for the captives and release from darkness for the prisoners, . . . to comfort all who mourn, and provide for those who grieve in Zion — to bestow on them a crown of beauty instead of ashes, the oil of gladness instead of mourning, and a garment of praise instead of a spirit of despair" (Selected portions of Isa. 61:1-3 NIV).

DAVID PRAYED FOR HIS BABY BOY

David fasted and pled with God to heal his infant son who was born to Bathsheba. He lay prostrate before the Lord. When the child died his servants wouldn't tell him because they were afraid of his reaction. Finally, when David noticed they were avoiding him, he asked if the child had died and they told him the truth. To their surprise, he got up, washed and ate. When questioned about his response, he told them that as long as the child lived, he had hope, but now there was nothing he could do. He announced, "I can't bring him back! Someday I will join him in death, but he can't return to me" (2 Sam. 12:23 CEV).

David refused to remain in the pit of despair. It was a painful period but he accepted the final verdict—his baby was gone. Later, he wrote that we may weep on our beds at night, but we can get up in the morning and look for joy. Solomon gave his bit of wisdom on the subject when he stated there are appropriate windows of time to express all kinds of emotions: weeping, laughing, mourning and dancing. These emotions are gifts for us to live life to the fullest.

Strong Emotions Cannot be Expressed in Words

It is interesting that the deepest emotions cannot be expressed in words. In great sadness and grief, we cry or mourn. When we are joyful, we shout and laugh. In the midst of pain, we may moan or even groan. We can express happiness by jumping up and clapping our hands. Nothing expresses peace more beautifully than a baby cooing with contentment. Though we stumble verbally in awkward situations, actions are often more expressive. No wonder the Holy Spirit makes intercessions with groanings that cannot be uttered.

When reading Jude, I read about praying in the Spirit. I thought and prayed about this. I felt God questioned me. "What language do you think I speak?" I knew He didn't speak only English. Then it dawned on me—God searches deeper to find attitudes that echo from our hearts.

OUR DARKEST HOUR

Our oldest son Rick dropped into the depths of depression—to the point that he became overwhelmed. On a couple of occasions he briefly mentioned his battle but we didn't pick up on the seriousness of it. We had no idea of the magnitude of his struggle . . . until. . . he took his life. After his death, we discovered poems he'd written that reflected, in part, what he had been going through. This is a verse from one of them:

> These days that last forever
>
> Don't last long in eternity
>
> I think I would feel better
>
> If only time would set me free

Shortly after we lost him I attended a retreat in Galveston. Our speaker asked us not to speak the next morning until we'd eaten breakfast. She suggested we take a walk and see if God would show us something we could share later with the group. I walked barefoot along the beach, dragging my feet in the sand, burdened with a heavy heart. When I stopped to watch the tide roll in, the presence of peace joined me on that beach. I spoke aloud, "Lord, it was such a miracle that You walked on the water." A thought washed over my mind: "Is it any less a miracle that you walk through the fire and aren't consumed, or that you walk through the water and are not overcome?"

God sent the message that it was possible to get past the hurt and pain of that loss. That emotional healing became more significant than any physical healing. Later, I ran across the Scripture I'd heard a portion of that day: "When you pass through the waters, I will be with you, and when you pass through the rivers, they will not sweep over you. When you walk through the fire, you will not be burned; the flames will not set you ablaze, for I am the Lord, your God, the Holy One of Israel, your Savior" (Isa. 43:2-3 NIV). In a very personal way, the Lord showed me He was with me in the pain I experienced. Thank You, Caring Father.

Time and again I felt I was in over my head, but even then I knew the Father stood by me. When the waters are rough and deep, I'm confident He'll keep me from sinking. When I find myself between a rock and a hard place, I'll climb up on that Rock for safety. The hard places in life will not crush me.

The earthquakes shaking our emotional world are often followed by multiple after-shocks. My husband was a psychologist and his first reaction when he learned of Rick's death was, "I'm quitting counseling. If I missed it with my own son, how could I ever help anyone else?"

Disbelieving, I stared at him. "Carey, that's exactly what Satan would have you do. He not only wanted to destroy Rick's life, he wants to destroy the effectiveness of the rest of our lives too." Yes, Satan designs his devious and evil schemes to effect as wide a range of devastation as possible. "Get out of my face, you conniving enemy!" I recalled that in the storms, the Lord is near. I cling to Him while dealing with the worst possible onslaughts.

Carey picked up his notepad and headed back to the office. He would continue to counsel and reach out to others with a message of hope. Satan failed to destroy us when he showed up in dark clouds with his wicked scheme. The Holy Spirit slowly lifted us above and beyond this dark period of our lives.

We received many heart-warming notes after Rick's death. One friend wrote she'd just moved into a new home, walked into the bathroom and the emptiness echoed loneliness. In her heart she felt, "This is how Carey and Louise feel. I need to encourage them."

Without consciously thinking about it, she began to hang curtains, towels and pictures. She placed knick-knacks around the room. The next morning, she walked in to find the sun streaming through the bathroom window. It made the entire room warm and inviting. She felt God said, "I will once again shine in Louise and Carey's lives."

THE NECESSITY OF FORGIVENESS

In spite of the encouragement, the devastating blow almost destroyed us. As I wrestled with the gut-wrenching reality, I realized that life's hardest struggles must often be met head-on with forgiveness.

There's some truth in the saying, "Beside every grave there are those who look for someone or someplace to unload the blame." I started with a soul-searching evaluation of my relationship with Rick and thought of times I'd disappointed him. I knew there were situations when I didn't act in his best interest because I was too preoccupied with my own struggles in life to extend him the love and support he deserved and needed. I loaded my own shoulders with a huge bag of guilt.

I proceeded to place a chunk of blame on Carey's tray for being an absent father and not taking him under his wing to train and mentor him.

I filled other buckets of blame and dumped them on our son's wife. Other platters were served to his friends who didn't return his calls when he phoned to tell them he needed to talk. I wrote down my 'justifications' for the unforgiveness I harbored toward each person. Realizing this was nonproductive, I laid my list aside and prayed for God's mercy to teach me the steps I needed to take to forgive every person involved. Not unlike peeling an onion, each layer of forgiveness produced tears as God exposed the hurts and asked me to trust Him to let them go.

I attended an Evelyn Christianson seminar on forgiveness a few weeks after Rick's death and tediously dealt with each person I'd blamed. It became an ongoing process of forgiving myself and others. God reminded me that the sacrifice of Jesus *was* sufficient to cover every sin of commission and omission.

I accused myself of being a bad mom, though I never intended to neglect or hurt Rick. I loved him before—I loved him then—I will always love him. It was sobering when almost six months after his death, Rick appeared to me in a dream one night and said, "Mom, please let me go."

Even in the excruciating pain of this loss of our son, there were lessons to learn. The very Scripture I'd asked them to use at his funeral became a part of our lives. "He comforts us when we are in trouble so we can share that same comfort with others in trouble." (2 Cor. 1:4 CEV).

We didn't know what to do—but we chose not to give up. We began to slowly move forward in reaching out to others who were hurting. As we supported others, God supported us.

I concluded I'd pretty well gotten past the worst by dealing with forgiveness until Carey and I attended a conference in Nashville—a full two years after Rick's death. On the final night of the conference, the speaker delivered a lesson on forgiveness. My mind kept flipping back to Rick's death. "Why, Lord? I think I've worked through forgiving every person involved."

Deep in my spirit I felt He confronted me. "You've not forgiven me."

I sat in shock. *What is this all about?*

After the meeting, we went home with the pastor for the night. The thought of forgiving God troubled me as the accusation kept sweeping across my mind. Could it be possible I *did* hold unforgiveness toward God?

As the others prepared for bed, they asked if I planned to stay up. "Yes, I have some business with God that needs attention."

They left me alone in the room and I hesitantly pulled out my notepad and pen. I always find it easier to express myself in writing. I began journaling while defensive thoughts kept rising to the forefront of my mind. "Lord, why do You say I haven't forgiven You? You've never done anything wrong—nothing you've done needs forgiveness."

"True, but in the recesses of your mind you've blamed me for failing to interrupt as Rick made final preparations to take his life." I caught my breath because I remembered all the times I questioned why God didn't intervene in those last moments. I laid down my pen as I rehearsed things I'd struggled with. "Lord, why didn't You prompt someone to call him on the phone even if it had been a wrong number? You could have had someone knock at the door or You could have even caused an earthquake. Merciful God, why didn't You do something?" I stammered—convicted of accusations I'd made. My heart squeezed tears up into my eyes and they overflowed their banks. These tears were a mixture of shame and pain seeping through the cracks of my broken heart.

Cautiously, I picked up my pen again and began to write slowly. "Lord, I do want to ask You to forgive me for blaming You—for whatever reason You didn't intervene." I paused at the impact of my next thought, but then wrote, "Tonight I'm choosing to forgive You for letting my son die." Tears streamed down my contorted face as I released this pent-up confession.

Within moments, the Lord spoke ever so tenderly, "And I forgive you for letting my Son die." I shuddered and wept with deep contrition. I *was* guilty. My sins most certainly played a part in nailing Jesus to the cross. Almost immediately, God wrapped a blanket of comfort around my trembling shoulders that had grown cold from wallowing in this chilling accusation. His arms enfolded me as I dealt with this hidden unforgiveness.

A heavy load was lifted from my shoulders that night. There will always be a deep hurt in my heart but it is no longer so raw and sensitive. God touched the untouchable.

§

I'm convinced forgiveness is essential and must play a major role in getting past trauma or hurt from the past. Moving forward frequently involves forgiving ourselves, others, and yes, even

God. Though the steps of forgiveness may be painful, they offer healing for our damaged emotions.

When dealing with trauma it's not unusual for instant replays to come crowding back in. I believe Satan invented the instant replay, complete with three-dimensional visuals with surround sound enhancement, smells and even vivid color. Shortly after Rick's death I wondered if there'd ever be more than five minutes when I didn't think of him. I struggled to resist the devil's assaults. He seemed to increase his attacks for a period but as I resisted him, he began to pull back from his dastardly attack—and eventually slithered away.

DIFFERENT TYPES OF TEARS

One form of tears may be those of regret. Most of us could easily spend an inordinate amount of time moaning and groaning over things we believe we should have done differently in life. As we grow older the list may well grow longer. Thank God, He's made provision. "You'll forget your troubles; they'll be like old faded photographs. Your world will be washed in sunshine, every shadow dispersed by dayspring. Full of hope you'll relax, confident again" (Job 11:13 MSG). It is amazing how God gives us the grace to turn loose of our guilt and shame, with the full assurance that He'll take care of all confessed sins of the past.

A good use of tears would be a sign of letting go. Hopefully, Christians bow in relinquishment as they turn things over to God. "Father, do it your way. Teach us to trust your mercy." When my sister Ruth's husband died and left her with two little girls, she said, "Don't ever let me blame God."

Another form of weeping comes from self-pity or the 'poor me' syndrome. I could hardly keep from chuckling when an older friend of mine would introduce herself with a whiney, "I'm just a pore, lit ole widder woman." She seemingly kept record of all the dismal things that happened so she could relate every pitiful condition she knew to all her friends and relatives. One day when we were visiting she bemoaned the fact that Runnels County, where she lived, had more cancer patients per capita than any other county in the state. After we left her house that day, my son Paul remarked, "Just think. They could erect a huge billboard in front of the court house with the proclamation, 'Runnels County, Cancer Capital of Texas'."

There are those who choose to be mournful. Jill*, a friend in Idaho, made it a practice to go to nursing homes and houses of shut-ins to play the piano for them. Her incentive was to cheer people by playing their favorite songs. Each time she visited one older woman, Jill would ask her what she wanted her to play. The woman would mournfully respond, "Play anything you like deary, just as long as it's sad."

I smile when I remember attending a wedding where the groom's mother walked down the aisle of the church with a huge box of tissue tucked under her arm. It looked as if she were announcing loud and clear—she hated to see her only child get married and move on with his life. I must remember, though, some tears at weddings are anticipated. When our daughter married in an outdoor courtyard, Carey lamented, "It was so hot that day my eyes started sweating."

Scripture tells us God collects our tears in a bottle. It puzzled me as to why God would store our tears. Perhaps there's an angel standing beside the pearly gates to hand our individual bottle of tears back to us. Maybe he'll ask us to pour them out with the admonition, "There will be no need for tears here."

There is a huge mural in Carthage, Missouri, where Samuel J. Butcher, the artist of *Precious Moments*, painted a picture of heaven with many little angels rejoicing in its resplendent glory. At the gate of heaven a little angel stands and hands out tissues to those about to enter and points to a sign nearby that announces, "No tears in heaven." Our compassionate God promises to take care of all our sorrows there. "They're his people, he's their God. He'll wipe every tear from their eyes. Death is gone for good—tears gone, crying gone, pain gone" (Rev. 21:3 MSG).

Some tears seem to be shed in anticipation. When a loved one is seriously ill and the doctor has forewarned they're going to die, tears may come early. My husband's physician told me two years before Carey died, "He'll not survive the cancer because it has metastasized all over his body." I did the bulk of crying before his life ended. I worked through many aspects of grief so that when the time came, it was almost a relief to know he'd finally been released from suffering.

I gained comfort when Carey told me a couple of nights before he died, "I felt the Lord held me in his arms all night." He believed God had given him a glimpse of His throne room. I was astonished but for some reason I didn't ask him what it looked like!

A few days before his death, I was in his room and reminded him, "For our twenty-fifth anniversary, we went to Hawaii. On our thirtieth, we went to Israel." My voice faltered, "You kept asking me where I wanted to go on this, our thirty-fifth anniversary and I never could make up my mind. Now it looks as if you're going without me."

There are tears of manipulation and even tears of joy, but I believe one of the God-given purposes of tears is to be an expression of sorrow distilled by His mercy. Now I know God's touch can heal the broken-hearted. Reluctantly, I offer my broken heart to Him to mend. I know that on my own, I don't even know where all the pieces belong.

In Scripture there is a Valley of Bacca. It was known as the Valley of Weeping. Later in Scripture, it was referred to as a Place of Springs. In the same way, we may find ourselves in a place of weeping but we can reach out with the hope that springs of Living Water will someday flow from that place.

THINGS TO CONSIDER

1. Should a person be ashamed to cry?

2. Is it a good idea to make a deliberate choice to limit your time of grieving?

3. How do you express your deepest emotions such as grief, joy and pain?

4. Considering your darkest hours, have you dealt with all aspects of forgiveness?

5. Is there anything for which you need to forgive God?

6. How do you show compassion to hurting people?

7. Do you ever cry tears of self-pity?

8. Can you accept God's forgiveness so you don't live with tears of regret?

9. Do you know people who use tears for manipulation?

10. Explain how tears are beneficial in the grieving process.

CHAPTER 21

WHERE REAL TREASURES ARE STORED

"Remember him—before the silver cord is severed…"

(Eccl. 12:6 NIV).

The old clock winds down and the ticking stops. One day the message from the brain will fail to trigger a heart-beat. Listen as you might, the thumping of the heart has grown silent. The life blood coursing through veins ceases— a sure sign that life in man or beast has shut down.

The umbilical cord is severed at the birth of a baby and pro-claims it's time for the infant to survive outside the womb. In a similar fashion, when the silver cord is severed, the spirit is released to live outside this earthly body. The connection by which the spirit has been tethered to the body is snipped. In God's scheme of things this disrobes us of our old earth-suit and it drops away so the beautiful spirit-being inside can be released to soar.

THE PROCESS OF BREAKING OUT OF THIS BODY

We see a correlation in Scripture between the planting of seed and the process of dying. In plant life the seed must fall to

215

the ground and die before the outer shell breaks open and exposes the embryo that brings new life. Until that time, it remains dormant; waiting to spring to life. One grain of wheat is never more than just that—until it falls to the ground and dies.

Our spirit is trapped inside a shell of flesh. At death, the silver cord is severed and the spirit is released to an abundant life. Like cutting the ribbon to celebrate a grand opening, the severed cord is snipped to open up a new life.

A New Look at Fractions

In school I had a mental block when it came to math. The only reason I took extra math classes was because my boyfriend was a whiz at math and he volunteered to help me with my homework. My puppy love for him faded and I never learned to love math.

My son, Paul, recently presented a beautiful concept about fractions. He suggested we use fractions to illustrate where we store treasures. The line between the upper and lower number can represent the Word of God dividing spirit and soul. It delineates what we've invested in heavenly assets and worldly interests. This line can be featured as the silver cord Solomon spoke of. Silver indicates something has been refined. A cord suggests something is bound. When the silver cord is severed, the refined spirit is no longer tied to this body.

Numerator - Heavenly Investments
Denominator - Worldly Investments

Let the top number of the fraction (the numerator) represent the spirit, where we lay up investments in heaven. A godly person adds to the value of that number by spending time reading, studying, meditating and praising God with joy and gratitude. His life is an on-going season of prayer. He's a wise steward with his money and generous in helping with benevolent work and spreading the gospel. He's the good neighbor for those in need and willing to help in whatever Christian endeavor the Lord leads.

The numerator also represents such things as obedience to God, humility, love and faith. Most of the things above the line reflect interests outside our own lives. They are evidence of love expressed toward God and others.

Let the bottom number (denominator) represent worldly things, where we invest in material things. We find that number enlarges as we place emphasis on self. Our mind, will and emotions pamper self-interests, wants and demands. The soul concentrates on acquiring more money, more power and prestige.

When the silver cord is severed the emphasis of 'me, my and mine' is gone. As valuable as the whole lot may be it cannot be traded for a ticket that grants access into the heavenly kingdom. Even a string of initials following my name doesn't impress God. A huge stash of wealth is worthless to a dead man— as worthless as Monopoly money shoved back in the box at the end of the game. All those things hanging on to the silver cord will drop away at death. Materialism will come crashing down—worth nothing.

In school we were taught that if the numerator (the top number) became larger than the denominator (the bottom number), the fraction would be labeled *uncommon* because its value would be more than a whole. When we focus on laying up treasures in heaven, they become of greater importance to us than things here on earth, and we too, become uncommon. We're different from the everyday person you meet on the street.

§

An acquaintance was worth ten million dollars. One day he announced, "I want to be worth a hundred million dollars." I looked at him in disbelief and ask, "What then?" He stared at me as if I'd asked a stupid question. A short time later he was charged with mail fraud and sentenced to two years in federal prison. The government seized all his assets. He came out of prison financially broke as well as a broken and humbled man. His wife said the experience was worth every penny he'd lost because it stripped him of his arrogance and pride.

"Don't love the world's ways. Don't love the world's goods, love of the world squeezes out love for the Father. Practically everything that goes on in the world—wanting your own way, wanting everything for yourself, wanting to appear important has nothing to do with the Father. It just isolates you from Him. The world in all its wanting, wanting, is on its way out—but whoever does what God wants is set for eternity" (1 Jn. 2:15 MSG).

Visualize a Brink's truck leaving a funeral procession and heading in the direction of the city dump with the dead man's possessions—no longer of any value to him.

WRONG EMPHASIS

In the little town where I was raised we had a n'er-do-well resident who bragged that one day he would be a very wealthy man as he had been named the sole heir of his aunt's estate. Year after year he waited. His aging aunt went into a nursing home that gobbled up the bulk of her money. When the aunt eventually died there remained only enough for him to buy a small house on the wrong side of the tracks. His hopes and dreams sank into oblivion and even the pitiful portion he received disappeared soon after, because of his early death.

§

We kept girls in Denver who were on probation from juvenile court. One girl's mother dropped by often and brought her gifts. One day she brought a gift and quickly left to go on her way. Her daughter threw the gift across the room and shouted, "Why can't she understand I don't want her stinking gifts. I just want her to show me she cares by spending time with me." Generosity is not measured by how much money we throw at someone. A gift without love is like paying your taxes; we pay them but don't enjoy it.

§

When I sold the farm I made a mistake in letting my broker invest most of my money in the stock market. I watched the Dow Jones fall day after day until one day I called my broker, "I'm bleeding to death. Help me." I showed poor judgment again by encouraging him to sell most of my stocks when the market was near the bottom.

I started thinking of where I could cut corners. Perhaps I should cut back on my giving. Then it hit me; Satan prepared a trap of fear and I'd fallen headlong into it. "Oh no you don't, Satan." In defiance I increased my monthly support of one missionary and contributed a sizable amount to another.

I felt at peace and announced, "I will not be intimidated by the devil and all his whisperings that I'm going broke. He's taunting me in an attempt to cause me to focus on the loss of money so I'll panic." I re-evaluated my situation. My only real concern is for my eternal investments to be solid and in a safe place. I worked through the process of forgiving myself for my lack of faith. I reaffirmed my trust in God. Then, I could sleep at night without tossing, turning and rehashing what possibly *could* happen.

WISE STEWARDS

George Pepperdine, who founded the Western Auto Stores, also helped establish the beautiful university that bears his name and overlooks Malibu Beach. At one point, when he struggled through a tough financial crisis, someone asked if he didn't regret giving so much money away. "No," he replied. "My faith is my fortune." I believe God smiles on those who cheerfully give with no second thoughts or regrets.

We're encouraged in this life to be wise stewards regardless of how little or much we've accumulated. Possessions aren't wrong or even unimportant but it is imperative to use them wisely. We can use and enjoy this world's goods while not becoming overly attached to them. God observes how trustworthy we are with our worldly possessions to determine if we'll be responsible with the riches of heaven.

REFINER'S FIRE

In Africa we visited a refinery where they were purifying gold. The caldrons were heated until the impurities floated to the top and were skimmed off. In the same manner, when the heat in life gets turned up, impure thoughts and attitudes frequently float to the surface. Genuine faith withstands the heat while God skims off the impurities.

During eternity I think we'll look back over our life on earth at God's refining process. We'll watch as He puts the finishing touches on us—through the hot and sticky situations we've been through.

Jesus keeps a safety deposit box with our name on it. It will ultimately reveal the total reward we have sent on ahead. The name "Jesus" is our pass word. "I pray that your hearts will be flooded with light so that you can understand the confident hope he has given to those he called—his holy people who are his rich and glorious inheritance" (Eph. 1:18 NLT).

LITTLE THINGS CAN BE OF GREAT VALUE

Right before my dad died he apologized that he'd not be leaving much of anything of value for his children. My brother corrected him, "Dad, you made sure we all got a college education and the legacy of the life you and Mom lived is worth far more than *any* amount of money."

We can't conceive the value God places on the seemingly small and insignificant things are valued by God. I remember Jesus pointing out the example of the widow's two mites, stating her gift amounted to more than all the rest. I predict we'll probably spend the first thousand years in heaven slapping our foreheads and exclaiming, "I didn't realize how much little things counted."

My dad was in a serious accident and burned so extensively he wasn't expected to live. My brother sneaked his four-year-old son into the hospital so he could see his beloved granddad. Dad gasped for breath as he greeted them. My nephew, Mark, spoke softly, "Granddad, I brought you something," and placed a nickel in his granddad's hand. Dad had tears in his eyes and struggled to whisper, "Thank you son, I'm going to put this in a special place and never spend it." He valued this little gift wrapped in a great big package of love. I believe God looks for that kind of attitude in our stewardship.

Surprises and Rewards

It's sheer joy to surprise someone with a special gift they have longed for. We came from a family of limited means. Mother had always wanted a wrist watch. One Christmas my older sister suggested Dad buy her one. He agreed, and suggested she go pick one out for Mom. Early on Christmas morning Mother opened the package. She literally jumped up and down and ran over to hug Dad's neck. "I never thought I'd have a watch of my very own." I think God gets excited as He prepares priceless surprises for His children.

The most important thing I want to hear will be God saying, "Excellent! You are a good servant. Since I can trust you with small things, I will let you rule over ten of my cities" (Lk. 19:17 NCV). In this statement I believe God not only refers to worldly goods, but to the use of talents, time, effort and the attitudes we maintain in life up until the very time when the silver cord is severed.

Compound interest has been referred to as the eighth wonder of the world. Nothing illustrates that better than that which God is adding to our account for us. As we invest time and money in the lives of others, God makes sure we get incredible dividends from our investment. Unlike the stock market, there's no speculation involved.

It's reassuring to know we can't out give God. We don't give to get, but there's a godly principle that as we take care of others, the Lord takes care of us.

Now is a time to take a look at our own lives. At best, we don't have many years until that silver cord will be severed. Anything we've accumulated will immediately belong to others. Everything we now see will vanish, and the unseen will become our only reality. God is beginning to give us more insight as to what true wealth is.

A CHRISTIAN'S IDENTITY

Our identity as Christians should be so unique that others will seek us out with a desire to discover the treasure we've found. We'll not only be uncommon among men but extraordinary in the sight of God. Be brave, be willing to be a part of the peculiar people driven by God's unseen Spirit to say, "NO" to instant gratification and be willing to wait in anticipation for what we are to receive in eternity.

There will come a time when our shelf life will have expired, our year model is outdated and replacement parts are unavailable. Our faith-based works will be on display as to what the Lord considered to be the true significance of our lives.

All the glittering seductions of this life will pale in the true wealth of eternity. Paul said: "I once thought these things were valuable, but now I consider them worthless because of what Christ has done." (Phil. 3:7 NLT). The beautiful spirit inside cannot be seen now, but will someday overshadow any package we've been wrapped in here. It's obvious that where we spend our time, money and effort is a clear indication of what we really treasure. Regardless of the value of our material goods, our lives should be rich toward God.

Times may be rough for a time here, but I love the statement Dr. Tony Compola expressed in a sermon about the crucifixion and the resurrection of Jesus when he shouted, "It's Friday but Sunday's coming"!

THINGS TO CONSIDER

1. Have you considered what it will be like when the spirit is released from the body?

2. How can you compare the body to seed—and brokenness as an indication that we are fully submitted to God?

3. How much do you trust God to be your True Provider?

4. How are you investing in eternal things?

5. What does it mean to be a wise steward?

6. Is it wrong to have great wealth? Explain. What are the dangers?

7. What is the attitude of your heart when you give?

8. Think of times you have surprised others with thoughtful gifts.

9. Do you spend too much time thinking about material things?

10. In this chapter a Christian was described as an uncommon fraction. What does that mean to you?

CHAPTER 22

MY FORGETTER WORKS OVERTIME

"...the golden bowl is broken..." (Eccl. 12:6 NIV).

P ossibly the golden bowl spoken of in Ecclesiastes refers to the brain. Why wouldn't the mind malfunction after all the battles and forces that have bombarded it over the years? The bowl—or source of our thinking—may not be broken but not all circuits work properly and the connections don't fire up as they once did.

WHAT DO THE EXPERTS SAY?

Research has shown that a majority of all illnesses can be attributed to our thought life, our genetics and environment. Recent genetic research indicates that it's possible even our genes may be affected by emotions. We, like Nehemiah, confess the sins of our forefathers and guard against some of their weaknesses that may possibly trickle down into our lives. About the only thing we can do about our environment is to distance ourselves from those who pollute the air with negativity, insults, crude remarks and profanity.

The primary thing we're left to deal with is our thought life. Since we live in a world of sarcasm and criticism, we have to stay on the alert and not to pick up on these thought patterns. "We are not fighting against humans. We are fighting against forces and authorities and against rulers of darkness and powers in the spiritual world" (Eph. 6:12 CEV).

The mind is the enemy's favorite battleground. When bad emotions are stirred up, they cause the brain to release chemicals that have an effect on our physical, emotional and spiritual well-being. Smidgens of Satan's lies attach themselves to truth in our thought life. They're like pesky barnacles—and all too often we allow them to stick. The result is distorted thinking. "Don't let anyone capture you with empty philosophies and high-sounding nonsense that come from human thinking and from the spiritual powers of this world, rather than from Christ" (Col. 2:8 NLT).

Anxiety affects our memory and our thought processes to the extent it produces a mixmaster of confusion. One day when I was stressed out, someone asked me to repeat what I'd just said and I replied, "Oh, I don't know. I wasn't listening either." Some refer to small lapses of memory as 'senior moments'. I'm afraid mine, like an irregular heart-beat, slips on a consistent basis.

Day after day I repeat, "Father, today give me the mind of Christ. Let me think godly thoughts. Renew my mind to the sharp status of by-gone days. Give me wisdom to know how to live today in a productive way. You are not a God of fear, but one of a sound mind." I continue to pray these Scriptures in hopes they will help ward off dementia.

Taking bad thoughts captive is a life-long process. It requires an ongoing effort to capture those little boogers before they, like chiggers, work their way under our skin and pester the daylights out of us. Negative thoughts carry something like a chemical virus that affects every organ of our body. Rehashing bad memories causes negative chemicals to pour into our systems.

When unforgiveness is stored in our mind it's like a trash bag filled with old garbage. It may contain the hot sauce of anger or the tartness and resentment of an old lemon. If it's not taken out it continues to rot. We often have to forgive the same thing over and over again. Bad memories cause us to wrinkle our noses every time we open that stinky bag. It's time to take them all out to the curb to be hauled away. We'll know the garbage is gone when we recall the incident without negative emotions seeping back in to stink up our lives. Though we remember what happened, it's almost as if it happened to someone else. We can shake our shoulders, hold our heads up and move on.

BURIED EMOTIONS

Our minds were designed to coordinate the body's major organs in an intelligent and coordinated process so they all operate as a well-oiled machine. The mind of Christ enables us to filter out the grime of negative thinking. "We use our powerful God-tools for smashing warped philosophies, tearing down barriers erected against the truth of God, fitting every loose thought, emotion and impulse into the structure of a life shaped by Christ. Our tools are ready at hand for clearing the ground of every obstruction and building lives of obedience into maturity" (2 Cor. 10:5 MSG).

Buried emotions are even more toxic. If we fail to deal with our problems, it's like trying to hold a beach ball under water. They pop up when we're tired or when we least expect them. Submerged emotions block endorphins that are released to produce joy and peace.

Emotions are God-given but it is our responsibility to learn to express them appropriately. With God's help, we acknowledge destructive emotions—face them and pray for God to show us how to release them. "Therefore confess your sins to each other and pray for each other so that you may be healed. The prayer of a righteous man is powerful and effective" (Jas. 5:15-17 NIV).

Some make the mistake of identifying themselves with their problems, diseases or shortcomings by making comments such as: "I'm such a dummy" or "I can't do anything right," or "my diabetes, my arthritis." Others blame someone else. "I got my bad temper from my father," and so on. All these put-downs lead to a lousy thinking and lousy moods.

I got upset over what I felt was a huge injustice. After a bad night of tossing and turning, I was so stiff the next morning I could hardly get out of bed. When I remembered my anger I repented and asked God to help me deal with it. Within twenty-four hours I was much improved and have not faced the same type of pain again.

Because we live in a fallen world we must accept that in life we'll not always do the right thing; others will not always treat us well and circumstances will not always go as we planned or expected. Any of these disappointments can suck us into destructive thinking which causes intellectual branches of our minds to begin to wither and shrink.

Aging is a time when our thought life may become filled with discouragement. Malfunctioning body parts become prime targets for Satan's pot shots of flaming arrows. He uses everything he can to discourage us, "You're not good for anything anymore and things are only going to get worse. What are you going to do when you can't take care of yourself?" God gives us the defense of His Word. I respond by telling the enemy, "I can do all things through Christ who strengthens me" (Phil. 4:13 NASB). This is not only a shield, but it smothers fiery darts.

INTELLIGENCE

Growing older doesn't mean we can no longer learn and increase our knowledge. It does take more effort but stimulating our mind wakes up sleeping areas of our brain whereas self-centered thinking causes our minds to shrivel. Our world grows larger as we become more involved in activities. We become more alert and our mind continues to expand.

Controlling our thought life makes our minds and bodies not only feel better, but we actually become smarter. Science has proven that even a brain damaged by years of toxic, negative thinking can begin to recover in a matter of days. God constructed our brains in such a way that our minds can be renewed. "Do not conform any longer to the pattern of this world, but be transformed by the renewing of your mind" (Rom. 12:2 NIV).

TOUCH

Hugs play an important role in staying healthy—both physically and emotionally. There are those of us that must face life alone—some because of death and others through divorce. Hugs are not readily available once our official hugger is gone.

I am blessed because I attend a church where members feel free to hug one another. I look for those who look like they need a hug and following that urge, both of us are blessed. My husband used to tell his audience, "Don't forget to hug the widows." Those who don't feel free to hug adults can look for children who need a hug. Visiting a retirement home often affords opportunities to hug many older people—who haven't had their quota for the day.

Some find that pets fulfill at least a part of this need but animals were never meant to replace human touch. It is sad to see families that cuddle and whisper sweet nothings to pets and neglect their own family members.

The 'failure to thrive' syndrome occurs in infancy when babies are fed and changed but are not cuddled, held and rocked. Some die from neglect. From the beginning we need human touch. Touch triggers our inner pharmacy that releases positive chemicals, reducing stress and even boosting our immune system.

When I worked in a psychiatric hospital, I occasionally found a patient curled up in a fetal position. Even the touch of another part of their own body seemed to offer a little comfort. The warm contact of skin on skin seems essential to our well-being. It's not unusual that when people are afraid, they often wrap their arms around themselves, press their legs together or perhaps cross their arms and hold on to their shoulders.

§

My son, Paul, was told a remarkable story when he worked as the clinic doctor in a nearby university. A minister visited him and told him about his daughter who had given birth to premature twins. They called him and said that if he wanted to see his granddaughters alive he should come to the hospital right away. The attending pediatrician didn't think either would live.

The grandfather arrived and asked permission to go into the nursery to place his hands on the tiny babies inside the incubators. The staff granted his request and he began to massage the babies, pat them and encourage them with soothing words, "Jesus loves you and gives you strength to live." He sang to them and the nurses watched as the babies began to respond by moving and breathing more easily. He continued to rub their little bodies. The pediatrician came in and suggested he continue the process. Once the babies rallied the grandfather went home to rest.

He had scarcely fallen asleep when the hospital called again. The babies were slipping away. He dressed quickly and hurried back to the hospital to resume the routine. This time the nurses recorded his voice so when he grew tired again, they took over massaging the babies while playing his recording. Remarkably, the babies not only survived but thrived.

The pediatrician dropped by the pastor's office years later. He told him, "I cannot tell you how many babies your recording has saved. Every time we have a baby in crisis, we turn on the recording and I have the nurses rub and pat the infants."

HUMOR AND INTELLIGENCE

Humor is energizing and healing. It gives us more flexibility in our thought life, as if the brain jumps and whirls in joy. Ideas come quickly, and we access other good thoughts when we're happy. When people brainstorm and laugh together at some outrageous suggestions they get excited over possibilities. Humor stimulates creativity.

Fun also motivates us. It is inexpensive, enjoyable and effective. It smashes toxic thinking. Even thoughts of fun play a vital role in maintaining health and energy. A person can be drooping and dragging when a friend calls to suggest they go out for an enjoyable outing. Typically, the immediate response is to feel energized and motivated as one looks forward to fun and relaxation. When we feel good it's easier to laugh; when we laugh, we feel better. It's a wonderful cycle.

Laughter has been shown to increase the ability to fight respiratory infections.

The good news is—if our thoughts are powerful enough to make us sick, they are powerful enough to make us well. Our thoughts, like an engine on a train, pull us up or take us down. We can always think of excuses for not getting out and being a part of enjoyable activities. "Those who wait for perfect weather will never plant seeds; those who look at every cloud will never harvest crops" (Eccl. 11:4 NCV).

Our Words

If we find ourselves thinking negatively, it's helpful to understand their potential for harm. Begin to express aloud positive ways you can deal with a situation. Set a moratorium on the time spent fussing and fuming over things. Speaking out loud stimulates our brains to think on a higher level giving us the extra input of auditory stimulation. Words must match what we think or our minds will get confused. Positive defenses are built when a Christ-like attitude is reflected in the things we think and say.

Refuse to accept that the 'golden bowl is broken.' Get up and get out. Laugh a lot, live a lot and love a lot. God can become our free, preventive health insurance. Let this be a time to open up your mind for the Lord to come in and glue the golden bowl back together. Our Savior carefully mends those things that are broken. He uses His love as the super glue that never fails. "God's son was before all else, and by Him everything is held together" (Col. 1:17 CEV).

Upon arrival in heaven, we will be told, "If you have ears, listen to what the Spirit says to the churches. To everyone who wins the victory, I will give some of the hidden food. I will also give each one a white stone with a new name written on it. No one will know that name except the one who is given the stone" (Rev. 2:17 CEV). This special name may mean that we have a very special place in the heart of God where only we can go. Could the name written on the rock possibly be His pet name for us throughout eternity?

Our minds are extremely powerful and can guarantee an overcoming walk with the Lord. Ask the Father to renew your mind until it is held together by a solid commitment to concentrate on thoughts that are in sync with His plans for our lives. I'd love for my name in heaven to be 'Joyful', 'Faithful' or 'Loving'.

THINGS TO CONSIDER

1. Do you have any negative thought-patterns that might affect your health?

2. Are you aware that your main battles are not against people?

3. Do you find it is difficult to think clearly when you're anxious?

4. Have you learned to pray about what others might see as insignificant?

5. How can you go about taking your thoughts captive?

6. Do you have any buried negative emotions?

7. Do you allow any of your problems to be a part of your identity?

8. Have you given up on learning new things?

9. If you are alone, are there ways you can fulfill the need to touch and be touched? (Some find grandchildren wonderful for this!)

10. Are you considering what a powerful influence your mind has over your physical, emotional and spiritual wellbeing?

CHAPTER 23

LEAKY FAUCETS

"...the pitcher is shattered at the spring..."(Eccl. 12:6 NIV).

AN EMBARRASSING PREDICAMENT

Uh oh. Could Solomon possibly be bringing up the sensitive aging condition with which I'm familiar? A pitcher is designed to hold water, right? In our physical body, the only thing comparable is a part of our plumbing system, or more explicitly, the bladder. Sadly, as a person begins to age, this organ may also begin to malfunction.

This container may not be shattered, but it's so worn out, it leaks. In his mid-nineties, my brother talked to me on the phone. Without an ounce of self-consciousness, he commented, "I have to wear diapers now." I've always thought of him as a little general because he is so dignified and proper. It pleases me to find he continues to retain his sense of dignity—even with this problem.

I went for an evening stroll with my sister, Ruth, and sister-in-law, Flo. Flo stepped in a hole and staggered as if she were drunk. We all giggled and Ruth burst out, "Look!" The three of us were standing in the middle of the street with our legs crossed. There was no need for anyone to explain. We knew the problem. This realization sent us into peals of laughter which made the situation worse.

I wracked my brain. Could anything purposeful come from this curse which assaults many of us that travel these last miles? No amount of wealth, prestige or power can exempt a person. Satan delights in humiliating us through these worn-out bodies.

§

I talked with a friend on the phone and she told me of her experience. "Last night I had the most embarrassing situation I've ever faced—it was awful!" She went on to tell me she'd gone out to eat with her family. Suddenly, she needed to go to the bathroom. She was mortified because she didn't make it. She cowered in the bathroom. After a time her daughter sent two granddaughters to check on her. My friend sent them back to get their mother while she cleaned herself up as best she could. Her daughter came to the restroom and suggested her mom follow her closely out to the car. My friend lamented, "I don't ever want to go out in public again. I am sooo ashamed."

"Wait!" I replied. "Think of how the devil wants you to respond to this. Doesn't he want you to be consumed with shame and humiliation? He'd like for you to just stay home and lick your wounds. Do the opposite of what he's trying to accomplish. Don't let him win!"

"I don't know whether I can do that or not, but you're probably right. I'm going to really have to pray about this so that it doesn't completely intimidate me."

The next day she called. "I went to the store and bought some protective underwear. Next time I go out I'll wear it so I'm prepared."

"Good for you! I'm convinced God is glorified when we remain steadfast through every trial." The apostle Paul was not referring to this problem but the scripture is appropriate: "I have learned to be content whatever the circumstances" (Phil 4:11 NIV). We're challenged to remain undaunted. When we're upbeat we don't unload a bad attitude on others—even when we have humbling encounters.

MORE PROBLEMS!

Still dealing with this distasteful problem, I'll throw caution to the wind and bring up another unpleasant aspect of aging. Older citizens often have a problem with gas, which does absolutely nothing to help solve the energy crisis and it contributes to air pollution! We clear our throats or shuffle our feet in an attempt to pretend the source of noise is coming from somewhere else. We're faced with dealing with bottom burping or noises resembling an old-fashioned coffee percolator. About the only thing we can do is to dismiss it with a nervous laugh. Though embarrassment is likely to linger we can refuse to let it control us.

I sense the enemy sitting nearby with a smirk on his face, whispering, "Now aren't you dignified, big shot? You can't even control your own body." He is intent on destroying our sense of self-worth. We refute his mocking and assert our God-worth. "No, despite all these things, overwhelming victory is ours through Christ, who loved us" (Rom. 8:37 NLT).

238

One way to defeat Satan in his dastardly plan is to resist re-acting in anger and humiliation. Shame, frustration and self-pity are no better. We recognize this as a part of the process of an old body breaking down, preparing for departure. Like an old dilapidated car, we need more than just a tune-up.

Though this body is wearing out, our attitude isn't obligated to wear down. We learn to face adversity with humility, rather than humiliation, with grace instead of grumbling. By God's grace, we will emerge spiritually and emotionally unscathed.

Taking a Different Look

God can even use this aspect of aging as a part of His plan to refine the inner man. It creates an opportune time to deal with pride. Pride is stomped in the dirt with flatulence and cracked pitchers. One definition of flatulence is "being pompous or self-important." Even a world class celebrity would have difficulty feeling so all-fired important if he has to deal with this problem in public. This may be a time to smile and say, "Oh well," and graciously accept this aspect of our transition.

Having taken a look at a leaky or worthless pitcher, there is a counterpart to this dilemma. Our spirit can be filled with the Living Water Jesus spoke of when talking to the woman at the well. It can be poured out, but it doesn't leak out. How beautiful to be a vessel to hold life giving water that overflows into the lives of others. This water was not designed to quench the physical thirst but it is a provision for satisfying the thirsting of the soul.

HOLD ON TO JOY

My husband, Carey, had a great sense of humor. He could laugh at himself in the face of monumental problems. When he was diagnosed with cancer and had to have a portion of his colon removed, he commented, "It's really no big deal. It's only a punctuation change. I used to have a colon and now I have a semi-colon."

In time the disease ravaged his body until he had to have a colostomy. Harry Brand*, Carey's friend and surgeon, told him, "If you go into remission, I will be able to reverse the colostomy." The problem was a hassle to deal with but Carey handled it well. A few months later he phoned Dr. Brand. "Is this Harry's Body Shop? I have a hole in my muffler and need a new tail pipe. How soon can I come in for you to fix it?"

"You crazy Looney guy, you'll just have to hang in there."

Sadly, Carey never went into remission to permit the surgery, though he held tenaciously to his ability to bring a chuckle or a smile to the lips of others. When he went in for chemo treatments, he often took roses or miniature candy bars to dispense among the staff and patients. One day he changed into his clown costume before going into the treatment room. It was another effort to lighten the moods of those lined up in chairs to receive their chemo.

One of the nurses told Carey, "It always makes me feel good when I see your name on my charts for the day." He told jokes and lifted the spirits of those around him. Soon others began to catch the idea and added their little bits of joy to that dismal place.

§

Older citizens need to seek opportunities to spread joy in the lives of others. We'll use the bubbling springs, flowing from deep within, to water them. We choose Living Water to nurture their good points—their flowers. We resist watering the weeds—their bad characteristics. The things we say can be uplifting, rather than degrading.

Perhaps rivers of Living Water represent joy from the Holy Spirit—flowing out of our innermost beings. We can make a concerted effort to look for things to laugh about. I'm convinced laughter is a strong defense against the enemy. Scriptures tell us that laughter is good medicine. Initially we may have to force it but we take seriously the mandate: "Always be full of joy in the Lord. I say it again—rejoice!" (Phil. 4:4 NLT)

§

Bring cheer to those around you. Give a cup of cold water in the name of Jesus. Surprise others with thoughtful little gifts and acts of kindness. We can tell clean and cheerful stories to make others laugh. (Nothing seems much more entertaining than to relate funny things about yourself.) Once Carey said, "Louise, you don't have to tell every dumb mistake you ever made."

"Perhaps not," I answered, "but when I do, I think others identify with me and are relieved that they're not the only ones to pull crazy stunts."

ANOINTED WITH JOY

This old body is worthless if it is broken with discouragement and can't hold Living Water. Look for those who are yearning for something that will quench their spiritual thirst. God can offer them something that is far more refreshing than mountain spring water.

Do you remember this little song? "I'm a little teapot short and stout. Tip me over and pour me out." If we are filled with love and joy, we can pour these into the lives of those around us. Bubbling joy is an open invitation for others to come and drink of this refreshing water. So what if our physical pitcher leaks? We have Living Water as an alternative. It is free and unlimited.

A Simple Clay Teapot

My niece, Claire, and I decided to go to China. She particularly wanted to visit the orphanage where six children had lived before they were adopted and became a part of her classroom in Texas. She loved the children and wanted to get in touch with their roots.

When we were in China, we visited a tea room where we were served different kinds of tea. Our hostess explained the rituals associated with each flavor. She served a jasmine tea in a simple clay pot explaining they always used the same pot to serve that tea as it absorbed more flavor each time it was brewed. The following night Claire had a dream in which God told her she was like that little clay pot absorbing more and more of the love of Jesus.

The next day Claire wanted to go shopping. She wanted to find one of those little clay teapots as a reminder of her dream. She purchased one at the market and brought it back to the

States as a souvenir. Shortly after we returned, she was diagnosed with cancer and died within a year. I was asked to speak at her funeral.

I took the little teapot from her home and explained how God had shown Claire she was like that little teapot, saturated with the love of God. As we left the funeral, it slipped from the bag and shattered on the ground. I was startled but later the significance hit. The teapot represented Claire's body which had also been shattered—releasing her spirit to go back to God who gave it. The brokenness exposed the flavor inside. The fragrance of God's love which flowed from within Claire will continue to live on, far beyond her short time here on this earth.

I miss Claire very much. Sometimes I get misty-eyed over this loss but I still take sips of the joy and love she brought into my life. The Living Water from her life still gushes forth and God is taking care of the tears. "For the Lamb at the center of the throne will be their shepherd; he will lead them to springs of living water. And God will wipe away every tear from their eyes" (Rev. 7:17 NIV).

§

Keep the welcome mat out, Lord. I don't expect it to be long. Fill me up, Lord—fill this thirsting of my soul. As I am filled, my cup of joy runs over and springs of Living Water splash all over those around me.

THINGS TO CONSIDER

1. How do you respond to embarrassing situations that happen in your life?

2. Can embarrassment be used to humble you rather than humiliate you?

3. How can you defeat Satan's attempts to upset you about these challenges of growing older?

4. How can you keep from wearing down when your body is wearing out?

5. How can you glorify God by remaining steadfast in these trying times?

6. What does living water mean to you?

7. Can you think of new ways to spread joy in the lives of others?

8. What do you think it means to come to Jesus to drink?

9. Are you becoming more and more saturated with the love of Jesus?

10. Do you know of someone who poured their life into another?

CHAPTER 24

PROBLEMS WITH THE OLD TICKER

"...the wheel is broken at the well..." (Eccl. 12:6 NIV).

This wheel could be symbolic of the heart, pumping life-giving blood throughout the body. The heart, our most vital organ, gives us life. If the heartbeat is stilled, life-sustaining blood grows stagnant and death is imminent as every cell in the body fades into death from lack of nutrients and oxygen.

The heart is nestled at the very core of our being. Astonishingly, a heartbeat is detected earlier than nine weeks of pregnancy. It begins to beat within the fetus even before the brain develops. The confirmation of a life can be celebrated when the doctor's stethoscope picks up the rhythm of a heartbeat inside the womb.

The fetus grows beneath the mother's heart, and with that close proximity it initiates the bonding process between mother and child. My daughter-in-law placed a recording of a heartbeat inside the crib of her newborn as a source of comfort—trusting the transition from beneath her heart to the outside world would not be so abrupt. The steady and ongoing heartbeat whispers, "I'm here, I'm here, I'm here."

THE HEART AND OUR EMOTIONS

The Bible identifies our heart as the cradle of our emotions, the wellspring of our feelings of joy and sorrow, excitement and fear, bitterness and peace, hate and love. The heart responds and transmits emotions to the rest of our body. We are instructed to guard this emotional center with utmost care. "Out of the overflow of the heart the mouth speaks" (Matt. 12:34 NIV). Whatever is bottled up in our heart will eventually spew out of our mouths. We must determine to keep our hearts from being hardened by the world, but rather changed within to become like the tender heart of God.

Wrong emotions emitting from our heart have an effect on our relationships with God and others. Scripture describes those who outwardly appear to be honoring God, but their hearts are not engaged. When we line up our body, soul and spirit with the Father, Son and Holy Spirit, we become pure in heart and the continuity of our lives is synchronized with the heartbeat of God.

Disgruntled people with bad attitudes expose their hearts sooner or later by the things they say. Evil thoughts conceived in the heart slither out—even between clenched teeth. The old saying, "Sticks and stones may break my bones but words can never hurt me," is grossly misleading, as wounds of the flesh heal much quicker and easier than wounds of the heart. God weighs our words carefully. "It's your heart, not the dictionary that gives meaning to your words" (Matt. 12:34 MSG). It is such a blessing for God to take a stony heart and give us one that is tender.

PHYSICAL MANIFESTATIONS

Our heart responds in different ways even when we just think of something fearful, peaceful or joyful. If you imagine someone giving you a large sum of money, your heart is apt to leap in excitement. Think of someone trying to break into your home on a dark night. No doubt your heart will pound with fear. Experiment by imagining different situations. Pay attention to how your heart reacts. The heart responds in an emotional way and our bodies follow suit in conjunction with the signals the heart sends out. When we feel fear in our hearts, our bodies may tremble and we get cold chills. The hair on the nape of our necks may actually stand on end.

When we feel great compassion or love we talk about our hearts melting or being tender. This can motivate us to hold a hurting person in our arms to comfort them. When others hurt we want to reach out and touch them.

Sometimes hearts become hardened when people are offended. Muscles tense, jaws and fists often clench. Hardened hearts may resist being touched by others' pain.

When we grieve, we typically refer to having a broken heart or a heavy heart, and tears often make us feel weak. On the other hand, when we are upbeat, we talk about being light-hearted and our bodies are energized.

SOME LOSE HEART

Our children were young, ages three, two and another in the 'oven.' We made the exciting decision to go to Japan as

247

missionaries. We decided to have a garage sale to raise money and dispose of most of our belongings. We set up long tables in the basement of our home, filled them with household goods and invited the people from church to come. Carey suggested we put a jar on one of the long tables and ask people to take what they wanted and put whatever they felt the item was worth in the jar. He assured me people would be generous because it was for a worthy cause.

After the sale, we stared in disbelief as we counted the money. We received only pocket change. My silver, pottery, wedding gifts— most everything was gone. We struggled against being downhearted and resentful. We loaded our children and the essentials we'd decided to keep in the car and headed for Texas. We went to a church that agreed to help us financially until we raised sufficient funds for our support—yet after six weeks they'd given us no money. Sleeping on the floor of the church building with our children and utterly broke, we felt abandoned. We were disheartened. Carey and I concluded that if the church was that negligent while we were in their midst we might well be left stranded in Japan with no money to come back home. We gave up the idea of being missionaries. We were heavy-hearted as we experienced the death of a vision.

For a while we surmised the enemy had blocked our way. Later I saw God's fingerprints. Carey decided to go back to school and finish his doctorate in counseling. He would spend the rest of his life ministering to others. God used the whole situation to get us in the position He planned for us.

A LIGHT OR ENTHUSIASTIC HEART

Carey, who later became my husband, sat in front of me at a college football game. Since I'd been a cheerleader, it was natural for me to be animated. Carey took me on a date a few weeks later and mentioned my enthusiasm. "I started to turn around at the game and say, 'Lady, if you lose your voice, you'll probably find it in my ear.'"

I like the feeling of being light-hearted and enthusiastic. Enthusiasm is an outgrowth of passion. It feels good to find things we can pour our hearts into—to be passionate about. Enthusiasm lifts us on the wings of excitement and expectation.

§

Often older people appear heavyhearted and lose their zest for living. I see those whose hope has drained from their faces leaving them with furrowed brows and down-turned mouths. Their expressions sag alongside their wrinkles. I'd much rather resemble my uncle who had crinkles encircling his sparkling eyes that deepened as the result of years of laughter.

Some older citizens contend they are justified in becoming discouraged because their bodies don't function properly any more. As age marches on, debilitating factors become snipers—shooting down one organ after another. There is a temptation to lose heart. When this begins to happen, it is a signal for us to look for things to be encouraged about—better still—be a catalyst to encourage others.

A heavy heart produces pessimism that is accompanied by a lack of initiative and energy, and it feels like a bucket of lead that presses down on our chest.

249

A Lonely Heart

Soon after a spouse dies, loneliness moves in as a haunting companion. Some widows or widowers compromise their convictions in an attempt to avoid being alone by immediately getting involved with someone else. Before it goes too far, it's good to get the counsel of godly friends. I'm aware of several who felt certain the Lord was leading them to marry very quickly after the death of a spouse. They went against the advice of others. Some later regretted that they'd let their loneliness overrule wisdom and counsel.

A lonely heart yearns for companionship. Finding activities to occupy our minds can be a diversion to keep us from experiencing extreme loneliness. When lonely feelings pester us, we need something to do. Go out to eat with someone, invite people in. Find others who are alone and plan things to do together. Keep a list of possible things you can do when you begin to feel lonely— things that will help you become lighthearted.

I find that when I isolate myself, the devil can walk all over me. God not only sent Jesus, but He also sent us the Comforter, the Holy Spirit, to be with us when we grieve our losses. We not only need spiritual help but we need people with skin on to keep us company. We search for those who have been through similar experiences so we can encourage each other and not give up on good fellowship.

I worked in a psychiatric hospital as a spiritual director. I visited with a patient who'd lost her husband and she moaned and grieved over his death. As I tried to comfort her by telling her I'd also lost my husband a number of years before, she turned to me and wailed, "Yeah, but mine is not coming back!"

Letting Go

Wise doctors sometimes suggest family members give their suffering loved ones permission to die. My friend June* prayed day after day that her critically ill mother would be healed. One day, while June was sitting by her side in the hospital, her mother rallied for a few moments and turned to her and said, "Please let me go." June was shocked when she realized her mom was ready to die and yet she'd been begging God to let her live. She thought for a few moments, took a deep breath and uttered, "Lord, if it's time for her to go, please take her."

Her mother's wish was granted within hours and she passed on to a better life. June allowed her mother's wishes to overrule her own heart's desire.

§

Mother asked to go to a nursing home after Dad's death because her hearing and eyesight were failing. She busied herself in helping set tables in the dining room, pulling weeds in the flower beds, working crossword puzzles and reading. She told us before she moved into the home, "I've already made up my mind I'll be happy there."

Mom had been in the home eighteen months when she went to the dining room to eat breakfast; she began to have chest pains and walked to the front desk to tell them. After the staff helped her lie down and call for an ambulance to rush her to the hospital, they phoned my sister and brother who lived nearby. They hurried to be with her in the emergency room. Mom turned to my brother and said, "I surely hope I don't mess up your plans to leave on vacation this weekend." She didn't. She was dead before noon. Even in the critical hours before death her heart was still concerned for others. My sister-in-law remarked, "Wasn't that just like Mom? Any time she decided to do something she never wasted time following through with her decision." Congestive heart failure had stolen her life but failed to touch her tender heart of love. Her new heart continued to stay in tune with God's love.

The day of her funeral, as we started to walk into the church building, a niece exclaimed, "Look! God sent flowers." We all looked toward the skies and were amazed to see a circle rainbow above the church. That beautiful phenomenon remained until we were starting to leave the cemetery. God comforted our hearts in a way we'd never expected.

Our broken hearts aren't like Humpty Dumpty's that "All the king horses and all the kings men can never put back together again." Our Savior carefully mends broken hearts. He uses his love as the super glue to hold us together. "He existed before anything else, and he holds all creation together" (Col. 1:17 NLT).

IF EVERYTHING GOES KAPUT

"My flesh and my heart may fail, but God is the strength of my heart and my portion forever" (Psa. 73:26 NIV). The heart cannot be recycled. The new heart God gives us is not powered by a pacemaker, but it is God's total heart transplant that lasts throughout all eternity.

THINGS TO CONSIDER

1. Think of those whose heart has been deceived.

2. Which emotion do you have the most difficulty controlling?

3. Think of ways a heart may control emotions in a bad way.

4. Do you make it a habit to ask to be led by the Spirit of God?

5. What kinds of situations are most likely to trigger bad emotions in you?

6. Describe the difference between a heart of stone—a hard heart and a heart of flesh—One that is compassionate and loving.

7. Describe the difference between a light heart and a heavy heart. How does your heart trigger what you think about?

8. Do you ever do things for others to get you mind off a broken heart?

9. How can God be the strength of your heart?

10. Can you imagine your heart beating in sync with God's?

CHAPTER 25

FROM DUST TO DUST

"...the dust returns to the ground it came from..."

(Eccl. 12:7 NIV)

God formed man from the dust of the earth and, in the end, man returns full circle. God created us to be biodegradable. We came from nothing, to become something, to return to nothing. Flesh and blood are expendable but this is no indication our lives are 'dirt cheap.' "For you were bought at a price, therefore glorify God in your body and in your spirit, which are Gods" (1 Cor. 6:20 NKJV).

Under my bed I find "dust bunnies" everywhere. I dare not disturb them. It could be the makings of a man. But then again, who knows whether he's coming or going?

FEET OF CLAY

We usually think of a person who says he has feet of clay as one who recognizes his human weaknesses. My feet of clay extend all the way up to my armpits. Though this body of weakness returns to dust, the spirit is totally alive and breaks free to be lifted on the wings of the Holy Spirit. Our bodies return to the earth as groundcover, but our eternal spirit returns to its roots, its place of origin. Our bodies decompose as dust, but our spirits are everlasting. Currently, God wants to fill these simple clay jars with great treasures.

Henry Wadsworth Longfellow writes, "Dust thou art was not spoken of the soul." It is reassuring to know that only the shell of man is expendable. Jesus paid with His life in order that our spirit might live with Him forever.

WHAT CAN GOD DO WITH DUST?

The book of Jeremiah tells a story about God doing a make-over with a nation. "This is the word that came to Jeremiah from the Lord: 'Go down to the potter's house, and there I will give you my message.' So I went down to the potter's house, and I saw him working at the wheel. But the pot he was shaping from the clay was marred in his hands; so the potter formed it into another pot, shaping it as it seemed best to him. Then the word of the Lord came to me: 'O house of Israel, can I not do with you as this potter does?'" (Jer. 18:6 NIV). If God can squash a nation and remake it, surely He can do the same with me. Many times, God has had to go with plan "B" in my life, because I've resisted His creative touch—to mold me the way He first planned.

God knows and understands the stages of life we go through and He stands ready to remold us at any age, even when we're old and have made bad choices. "For He knows how weak we are; he remembers that we are only dust" (Psa. 103:14 NLT).

God has had me on the potter's wheel for well over three score and ten years. Despite stiff joints, I want to stay resilient in the Master's hand. Let Him shape me as He will. Perhaps the Water of Life will keep me pliable.

Don't Argue With God

Have you wondered why God created us with the type of personalities we have? We trust God in that He knew perfectly well how to put us together and give us the talents He intended for us to have. How foolish to quarrel with the Creator, as if we think He doesn't know what He is doing. This would be like trying to tell Michelangelo how to paint.

We need to look in the mirror and thank God for our features—even those we don't like. Instead of grumbling and complaining, we ask the Father for His grace to shine through our imperfections. "And the parts we think are less honorable, we treat with special honor" (1 Cor. 12:23 NIV).

When my son, Paul, was in the first grade, some of the children were making fun of a classmate who had a physical defect. The teacher interrupted their mocking and explained that everyone has flaws. Paul raised his hand and asked to show the children something different about his feet. The teacher allowed him to come to the front of the room while his classmates gathered around. He took off his shoes and showed the children toes on each foot that were webbed. The children recognized that each person is different and that they were to accept each person—just as they were.

Now Paul laughs, "My grandfather had webbed toes on one foot—mine are webbed on both feet. While the webbed toes on my feet allow me to swim well—my grandfather could swim circles around anyone!"

§

I'm not as smart or talented as some of my brothers and sisters. Both my sisters were valedictorians of their high school graduating classes, I was not. My brother was the 'fair-haired' gifted artist and leader in the school and community, but I wasn't. When I finally accepted the unique way God had made me, I developed my own potential and looked to God for my self-image.

I'm so thankful God gave all of us the same message of hope through His Word and His Son Jesus. He's not partial to anyone. There's a special place for each of us to work in His kingdom. God uses all types of individuals to spread His Word and His love.

Ken Starr, president of Baylor University and former Federal Judge and Solicitor General, told about an experience he had in Washington D.C. He spoke about a young man with Down's Syndrome who operated the elevator in his building. Every day he greeted Ken with a huge smile and said, "Good morning, Judge, have a wonderful day!" This man set the tone for the day. Ken stated; "It saddens me to find that now more than 90 percent of children with Down's Syndrome are aborted."

SEED NEEDS GOOD SOIL

The Word of God is sometimes compared to seed. Sometimes that seed falls along the path and gets trampled. There are countless millions who have no regard for God's Word and needlessly tromp it underfoot. The average Christian home has four Bibles but it would be interesting to know how many are read on a regular basis. We treat our Bible as if it is of little value when we fail to study and follow its teachings. *Lord, don't let our lives become like the dust on the Bibles on our shelves, because we're not an open book with our faith. Pick us up Lord. Dust us off and use us.*

When I smuggle Bibles into a foreign country, I hope they don't get confiscated and destroyed as I go through Customs. The people waiting for these Bibles are good soil. One of my friends in that country has a Bible her mother hand-copied in its entirety so she could have one of her very own.

There are seeds that fall on hard ground. With a little moisture the seed may sprout but then wither away. We need the water of the Holy Spirit to bring the Scripture to life. Seeds that have been found in the tombs of the pyramids have been taken and planted in good soil and watered. Surprisingly the seeds have spouted, grown and produced a crop. This is a reminder that even at the eleventh hour of life a seed that has lain dormant for years can still take root and grow.

§

A couple of years ago an older woman from church approached me and asked me to pray that her husband would make a commitment to the Lord. We prayed and over a year later she came to me and asked if I remembered our prayer. I did. She said, "My husband became a Christian a few months later. A short time afterwards he died but he had developed a strong faith. I had prayed for him for seventy-five years." She had cultivated the soil in her husband and good seed finally took root. Her prayers had not been in vain.

In the natural world, some fruits ripen in late fall or early winter. I pray that during the late seasons of life some will receive the latter rain of the Spirit and still produce great crops.

Not only have we been given the responsibility of being caretakers of the seed we're commissioned to carry that seed all over the world searching for good soil. We've all been entrusted with God's Word to plant and water, while realizing that only God can make it grow.

Personally, I feel my main gift is to water, nurture and encourage others. I like to take struggling Christians under my wing to mentor them. I want to teach younger Christians how to pull out weeds of anger, shame and unforgiveness.

§

During the fifteen years I lived at the retreat center I watched many people experience beautiful encounters with God. Jill* hoped to reconnect with God in the kind of relationship she'd had in earlier years. As she stood on the porch of the Casa, our Golden Retriever Sassy came to the gate and barked. A moment later Sassy trotted up to her side briefly and then went back to the gate and barked again.

Jill thought, *This is strange, but I think the dog wants me to follow her.* She walked over and patted Sassy and then followed her deep into the woods. She came upon a wooden cross we'd constructed with a bench next to it where people could sit and meditate. When Sassy lay down among the weeds by the cross a chill went down Jill's back. She felt God whispered, "That's your life—all full of weeds." She got up and went over to lie at the foot of the cross and cried as she identified and pulled the weeds she realized she'd allowed to grow in her life. Her life had been good soil but she'd failed to tend godly plants so weeds had taken over. When she finished, she felt a great weight lifted from her shoulders because she'd pulled those weeds that had strangled God's place of priority. We, too, are like soil—either receptive to the seed of God's Word or we allow it to be choked out by distractions of the world.

§

"For you have been born again, not of perishable seed, but of the imperishable, through the living and enduring Word of God" (1 Pet. 1:23 NIV). Young women produce seed that is capable of reproducing a baby. However, there comes a time when aging stops this cycle. But the seed of the Word of God, implanted in one's heart, can continue to reproduce life that lives throughout eternity.

When this old shell returns to dust—I'd like to think this clay pot has been shaped and used for the purpose God intended—either filled to the brim with the seed of the Word, or filled with water to nurture tender plants that will continue to grow and bear fruit long after we've returned to dust. When this old body drops away and returns to dust we have the opportunity to come to the Father with clean hands and a pure heart.

THINGS TO CONSIDER

1. Explain some of the ways the spirit is different from the earthly body?

2. In what areas do you think God is trying to reshape you now?

3. Do you ever feel you are too old to change?

4. Have you ever wondered why God made you as He did?

5. Can you think of how God can use something you don't like about yourself to accomplish something good?

6. Have you ever seen God use an unlikely person for a great purpose?

7. Do you ever feel cheated because of the things that have happened in your life?

8. Why should we never stop praying for someone to be saved?

9. Can you think of someone you need to pray for to become a Christian?

10. Are there weeds in your life you need to pull out?

CHAPTER 26

RELEASING THE SPIRIT WITHIN

"...the spirit returns to God who gave it" (Eccl. 12:7 NIV).

S oon the wheel will be broken at the well, the silver cord will be severed and the spirit will vacate this old body. Similar to a hermit crab, our spirit occupies this shell for a while but God did not create it to live here permanently. It is set free to be transported faster than the speed of light to live forever in the presence of the great I AM. This old body will have served its purpose and is ready to be discarded. But this is not true of the spirit.

DIFFERENT KINDS OF SPIRITS

We cautiously examine the Scripture making sure we are filled with the right kind of spirit. There are good and bad spirits. There are deceptive and lying spirits, vile and evil spirits and those that are unclean. But, as children of God, we have access to His Holy Spirit that can fill and empower us, guide and comfort us.

We are given the Holy Spirit at baptism but Luke tells us we can also ask for it. "Even though you are bad, you know how to give good things to your children. How much more your heavenly Father will give the Holy Spirit to those who ask him!" (Lk. 11:10-13 NCV) As we respond in obedience to the Father, we find His Spirit living in us as evidence that we are citizens of a heavenly kingdom.

We ask God to help us live in such a way that we do not grieve or quench the Spirit. We long for every possible resource to live in a way that glorifies the Lord.

Nothing is more important than preparing our spirits to live forever. God helps us by lavishly providing us with His Holy Spirit to lead us into all Truth. His gift equips us to live far beyond what we could ever do alone. "Those who have lived the right way will walk into resurrection life" (Jn. 5:28 MSG).

§

Since Celia was moving away, the young people at church gave her a farewell party. A friend handed her a card that read, "I really haven't gotten to know you as well as I'd like, but over there on the other side, I'm reasonably sure there's a grassy slope, just beyond the river. Just after the sound of the trumpet, meet me there. We'll get better acquainted and we can visit whenever we want." Celia's light shines brightly here but it will rise like the noonday sun in eternity.

§

The time of judgment is coming when the books will be opened. One book contains the things we've done in this life and we'll be judged according to those records. We'll stand before Almighty God ready to give an account for every deed and every word. We thank God that when those books are opened there will be page after page that is blank because we've confessed the sins that were once written there. Because of Jesus, He blotted those sins out—never again to be held against us.

I think we already know if we'll stand in the winner's circle because we accepted Jesus as our provision for forgiveness. On that day there will be a second book that will be opened which contains a list of God's adopted children. The names in that book will be written in indelible ink by the finger of God. Nothing can erase them.

No Target for Satan

Remarkably, when the spirit slips through these cracked and broken vessels, it flies away as silently as butterfly wings and carries none of the trappings of this earth with it. "For instance, we know that when these bodies of ours are taken down like tents and folded away, they will be replaced by resurrection bodies in heaven—God made, not handmade—and we'll never have to relocate our tents again" (2 Cor. 5:1-2 MSG).

Satan cannot afflict a dead body with pain, disease or weakness. When someone dies, friends and family may consider it a defeat—that the person has fallen prey to the devil's schemes. Initially, it may look as if Satan has won the prize package. But the enemy will discover the contents are gone. He's left holding an empty container of dirt filtering through his wicked fingers. That which has been born of the spirit cannot be touched or seen by any demon of hell.

Soon we will be out of here and the enemy can no longer harass us. There are no emotions left in the body for him to torment. Only the fruit of the Spirit survives and that fruit departed with the great exodus.

THERE IS A TIME TO RELEASE THE SPIRIT

As Carey's health declined we'd done everything we knew to stop the spread of the disease but we determined to trust God to hold eternity in His hands. We were forced to bow in humble submission as we watched Carey graduate summa cum laude and accept the invitation to 'come on home.' "So friends, confirm God's invitation to you, his choice of you. Don't put it off; do it now. Do this, and you'll have your life on a firm footing, the streets paved and the way open into the eternal kingdom of our Master and Savior, Jesus Christ" (2 Pet. 1:10 MSG).

When that time comes, we'll concede; nothing we endured has been too great a price to pay. No pain has been too unbearable, no struggle too difficult, no trial too long and no sorrow too deep. All struggles combined are as nothing compared to the glorious reward waiting for us.

The shroud of death and all it implies will have dropped away to be replaced by a robe of righteousness. There will be no need to bemoan what we have been, for we will discover what we have become. We loosen our clenched fists that have held on to this life in order to grab hold of something far better.

Shame and regret will be banished from our memories as we wash our robes in the blood of the Lamb. Pain will evaporate in the light of the Son. We will rise up in blessed relief—knowing the serpent has been cast down. He will never again approach us in an attempt to rob, kill and destroy anything good in our lives. He's led us astray for the last time. We'll no longer be deceived by his schemes.

Time and age will no longer cause us to stoop. The weight of all our concerns and the cares of this world will be permanently left behind. We'll be rid of all burdens. We'll stand tall and straight and our strength will be sufficient forever. Rather than be cowed by fear, our whole being will ripple with bold confidence. This earth and its troubles will never again shake us.

We will witness and hear the reverberating voices of those bowing before the throne throughout eternity praising God, "Holy, holy, holy is the Lord God Almighty. He was, He is and He is coming" (Rev 4:8 NCV).

§

On that day our spirit will be set free and the old cocoon gray in death and crackled by age can no longer restrain the spirit from returning to God who gave it. The wind of the Holy Spirit will scatter the dust that remains and all the dirty limitations that have been imposed on this mortal body.

Faith will erupt into reality. Hope will burst forth into full possession of more than we ever dreamed. The updrafts coming from the wind of the Spirit will continue to lift us higher.

Every burden will have been lifted from our shoulders. No heart will ever be stilled or broken. Can you imagine any greater freedom than being free from fear, free from financial concerns, living in the land where God owns the cattle on a thousand hills?

There will never be any limits or shortages of anything good. Even our thought life will be pure. There'll be no jealousy of those who are permitted to sit close to the throne. We'll simply rejoice in the mercy and grace our Father has shown to us, understanding the depth of His love for each individual. A new power is in operation. "The Spirit of life in Christ, like a strong wind, has magnificently cleared the air, freeing you from a fated lifetime of brutal tyranny at the hands of sin and death" (Rom. 8:1 MSG).

"So don't you see that we don't owe this old do-it-yourself life one red cent? There's nothing in it for us, nothing at all. The best thing to do is give it a decent burial and get on with your new life. God's Spirit beckons. There are things to do and places to go!" (Rom. 8:12 MSG)

We look forward to the time when our spirits will be free—free indeed.

THINGS TO CONSIDER

1. Would we be so concerned about this body if we realized the real significance of the spirit?

2. What are you doing to produce more of the fruit of the Spirit in your life?

3. Explain how you have seen bad spirits at work in someone's life.

4. Have you thought about how wonderful it will be when Satan will no longer be able to harass you after your spirit leaves the body?

5. What does it mean to have a free spirit?

6. Do you believe that eternal life is worth far more than the price we have to pay for it?

7. What do you hope to understanding in heaven?

8. What will it be like to have no cares in heaven?

9. What pain and trouble are you excited about not having to deal with in eternity?

10. What does it mean to you to realize that every time you confess a sin, God totally erases it from His record book and never remembers it again?

CHAPTER **27**

THE MEANING OF IT ALL

"Meaningless! Meaningless!" says the Teacher. "Everything
is meaningless!" (Eccl. 12: 8 NIV).

W hen Adam and Eve sinned in the Garden of Eden
they were sentenced to live in the clutches of aging
and death. This silent destroyer began to claim his
victims from one generation to the next, until now he's staring
at some of us as we enter this stage of growing older. Satan takes
advantage of this curse and sneers as we struggle with bodies that
are wearing out and breaking down. If we look at our life from
just a physical viewpoint, it is meaningless.

This may well be the most challenging time of our lives but
God never intended for it to be meaningless. Regardless of what
happens to this old earthly body, we can be confident our compassionate God is not playing a cruel joke on his older children
by creating sagging body parts, wrinkles and malfunctioning organs. God may allow this to be a humbling experience, but He
never intended for it to be humiliating.

METAMORPHOUS

God takes what Satan intended to be a devastating blow and uses it for a metamorphic process - a time of developing something beautiful on the inside - while this old gray cocoon is drying up and dropping away. Envision the spirit as a proverbial butterfly, developing inside and growing more beautiful every day.

A light bulb switches on above my head—Scripture come alive. "So we're not giving up. How could we! Even though on the outside it often looks like things are falling apart on us, on the inside, where God is making a new life, not a day goes by without his unfolding grace" (2 Cor. 4:16-17 MSG).

Concentrate on what really matters in this transmutation. Hold steady while God puts the finishing touches on the breathtaking spirit glowing within. This is our season to shine from the inside out. The transparency of our lives makes the validity of our love for God and others crystal clear.

During the transformation inside a cocoon the caterpillar sends out antibodies in an attempt to destroy the butterfly. It hampers its growth somewhat but ultimately the new creature grows stronger until the caterpillar melts into a soupy nutrient upon which the butterfly feeds. Could not the Lord use our bodies to nourish a beautiful spirit within? Even as this old shell grows old and crackly, we can remember the wings of victory are unfolding.

§

One day my twenty-three-year-old niece Celia came to me and said, "Open your mouth."

I opened it a bit.

"Open it wide." Though I didn't understand, I complied.

"Ah, you're beautiful in there too."

Thanks, I needed that.

Life would be meaningless if, when we leave this planet, blank eyes were left staring at nothing of significance we've left behind. Thankfully we still have time to touch others' lives by lifting them up. The bits and pieces of things we say and do strongly influence others. What would people miss if you were suddenly whisked out of the picture? If our concern has only been on physical bodies and material things we'll end up as mortals whose value depreciated with time. But if we dedicate our lives to being servants of God, we'll find ourselves reaping eternal dividends. We can stay cool in spite of hot flashes that keep distracting us.

Remember the inspiring movie, "It's a Wonderful Life"? Jimmy Stewart was taken back in time and see how different things would have been if he'd never lived. Would there be an empty void if we'd never touched people's lives? Is the world a better place because of our existence? "They share freely and give generously to those in need. Their good deeds will be remembered forever. They will have influence and honor" (Psa. 112:9 NLT).

There are many contributions we can make at this stage of life that can impact others for good. I'm not talking about humongous accomplishments or stashes of wealth but rather, sprinkles of joy and showers of blessings overflowing from a heart of love toward God and others. We determine to impact the culture rather than allowing culture to control us. God has designed this powerful force to come from the inside and flow out to the world.

In order to prepare for a meaningful future, it is important to create a meaningful today. Begin to make mental notes of ways to bless others. Consider how much it would mean if we took a few minutes every day to express gratitude to God and others for the way they have enriched our lives. Send a note, an e-mail or give someone a phone call. "Yes, you will be enriched in every way so that you can always be generous and when we take your gifts to those who need them, they will thank God" (2 Cor. 9:11 NLT).

§

Surprises are especially meaningful. My good friend Sarah had an old, beat-up chair in her attic. It had been a gift to her aunt from students and teachers when she served as a school principal during World War II. Sarah's daughter, Charla, had chosen it as the one thing she wanted when her aunt died. The chair fell out of a truck in a move and was broken in several pieces. Not wanting to dispose of it, they put it in the attic and subsequently forgot it for decades.

Charla became a school principal. While she was on vacation, her mother took the chair, had it restored, and placed it in her office at school—for her to discover when she returned from her trip. Charla wept in gratitude over her mother's thoughtfulness in restoring this sentimental treasure.

§

My husband kept a special file folder with encouraging notes others had written him. He got them out on days he felt discouraged. I found these after his death along with silly notes and poems I'd written him over the years.

Far too often I've been guilty of thinking of things I should do and say and somehow keep putting them off, never getting around to doing them. One day my son, Paul, said, "Mom, somehow I get the feeling you think you get brownie points just for thinking about doing nice things." Ouch! Guilty as charged.

It is time to give our attention to what God would have us do right now. Yesterdays may be filled with lost opportunities—but today gives us a chance to live so there are no regrets.

ARE THERE THINGS WE NEED TO LET GO?

Al* came to the retreat center and sat with us outside on the deck for morning devotional. He told us how others had taken advantage of him and misfortunes had plagued him in his business. He was convinced— the world had not been fair to him. We acknowledged that the world is often unfair. "The world is unprincipled. It's dog eat dog out there! The world doesn't fight fair. But we don't live or fight our battles that way—never have, never will" (2 Cor. 10:3 MSG).

As Al shared his struggles I was distracted by a dead leaf dangling from a spider web above his head. When I could no longer sit still, I got up and went over and yanked it down, apologizing for my strange behavior.

After the devotional Al went back to the Casa, one of our retreat houses, to sit outside on the glider. A gust of wind blew a shower of leaves in front of him. He observed how lifeless the leaves were—all crackly and brown. He saw a correlation between the leaves and his life and came to the conclusion there were a lot of dead leaves from his past needing to be blown away.

273

He symbolically lifted each issue up and asked for the wind of the Holy Spirit to blow them out of his life.

He looked at the tree shedding its leaves and it reminded him that old leaves had to drop in order to make way for new ones to grow. Al understood. It was time to start building new experiences. "Your old life is dead. Your new life, which is your real life—even though invisible to spectators—is with Christ in God" (Col. 3:3 MSG).

§

We can redeem the time by concentrating on a meaningful life today. We'll discard dead issues. We're not just biding our time. Our lives here are not a dress rehearsal, but we're on stage performing before a live audience. It's imperative to make these remaining days meaningful for those watching. We don't have to lament over times we've messed up in the past. This is a new day and we can still utilize the marvelous gift of life God has given us.

Rather than our efforts being meaningless, we determine to work with God in order for our lives to be fulfilling and worthwhile. "Blessed rest from their hard, hard work. None of what they've done is wasted; God blesses them for it all in the end" (Rev. 14:13 MSG).

MAKE LIFE MEANINGFUL FOR OTHERS

Eddie spent his life reaching out to underprivileged children who lived on the streets of New York City. He traveled across the nation to raise funds so these children could have an opportunity to get out of the city and go to a fun place where they'd also be given hope by learning about Jesus.

When Eddie drove down the streets on the East Side, he honked the horn of his old bus. Children ran after him as if he were the Pied Piper. He handed out brochures to advertise two weeks of free camping which would get them out of the slums into the glorious countryside.

He visited us in Denver on one of his cross-country treks and commented, "It will be so good when God calls me home. I'm worn out and ready for a long rest." When we went out to the car the next morning to see him off, Carey gasped as he looked at his tires. "Eddie, those tires are worn down to the tread. You'll never make it home on them."

Eddie sighed. "The Lord sent me on this mission and He knows I don't have money to buy tires. I'm counting on Him to see me home."

He wrote us afterward. "The day after arriving home in New Jersey, I went out to my car and found two tires were flat." Eddie worked hard for quite a number of additional years and then one day God granted his wish and took him home to rest.

I look forward to meeting him in heaven. He'll probably be followed by a whole passel of children who will be doing cartwheels along the banks of the River of Life. I can almost hear his hearty laughter in the distance as he urges them, "keep on running." Until the end, Eddie's life remained meaningful as he touched countless hundreds of children's lives.

STAY FAITHFUL TO THE END

We determine to live each day secure in the fact that if it were our last it would be fine. I still have projects I'd like to finish but I hope that's true when the last trumpet sounds. Slowly, resolutely we march to the sound of a distant drummer knowing we draw closer to our destination every day. We'll not give up the hope of completing our purpose here victoriously.

It will be wonderful to hear Jesus say, "Come, you who are blessed by my Father, take your inheritance, the kingdom prepared for you since the creation of the world" (Matt. 25:34 NIV). This will be what Paul Harvey often referred to as "the rest of the story." This time will be far from meaningless. This 'meaningless' world will no longer be listed as our permanent residence. We've prepared to move into a meaningful country of incomparable joy and beauty.

I can't say this road I've traveled has been easy, but I can assure you that following Jesus is gloriously fulfilling. As we fit into God's plans, our mouths will be so filled with laughter our tongues will taste its sweetness. Our hearts can continue to be vessels of peace, pumping love and hope along the way. No one can convince me this journey has been meaningless!

When we reach the other side, life will never have been so real, light never will have been so pure or joy so complete. "Now we see but a poor reflection as in a mirror; then we shall see face to face. Now I know in part, then I shall know fully, even as I am fully known" (1 Cor. 13:12 NIV). The transformation will be complete. Meaninglessness will have been transformed into meaningfulness.

THINGS TO CONSIDER

1. Has the enemy chosen to use aging and disabilities to discourage or defeat you?

2. How can you compare the spirit developing inside to that of a butterfly developing inside a cocoon?

3. Are you able to envision God working inside to develop a beautiful spirit?

4. Can you see God's purpose in the outer shell (our body) having to drop away in order to release the spirit within?

5. What little gifts can you give to those around you?

6. Can you think of a surprise you might give someone?

7. Is it difficult for you to follow through with ideas you have to reach out to others?

8. What could you do today to make life more meaningful for someone else?

9. Do you tend to only be concerned about your own problems?

10. What would help you switch from things in your life being meaningless to make them more meaningful?

CHAPTER 28

OUR HIGHEST PRIORITY

**Solomon concludes his discourse on aging
with a profound statement:**

*"Now all has been heard; here is the conclusion of the matter:
Fear God and keep his commandments,
for this is the whole duty of man" (Eccl. 12:13 NIV).*

When Solomon targeted the highest goal for our lives, he cautioned us to look to Almighty God for guidance rather than depending on our own wit or even on the great minds of the ages.

God's laws hang from a golden thread of love running throughout the Bible. The substance of God's mandate is to love others as much as we love ourselves. Love includes reverence and honor of God and respect for all His children.

In preparing to come before our Father of love, there'll be no need to shop for appropriate clothing. We'll be given a robe of righteousness purchased by the life and death of His Son, Jesus. The blood of Christ saturates the warp and woof of this priceless garment. Like Joseph's coat of many colors, its many features represent an incredible provision from a loving Father.

Not only does God furnish the robe of righteousness, but He plans an extreme make-over for our bodies. He prepares us to march into that eternal city to reign over principalities and powers—with wisdom and strength. We practice now by reigning over our attitudes and selfish interests.

GOD DECIDES THE TIMING

An ancient Jewish custom dictated that a young man prepare a place for his new wife. The father watched for the appropriate time to tell his son, "NOW, go get your bride." Even now, Jesus waits for the Father to send Him for the church, His bride. As a part of this bride of Christ, we experience great excitement as we anticipate His coming to carry us across the threshold and surprise us with our mansion in heaven.

We are preparing for this joyous occasion, getting cleaned up—literally on the outside, but symbolically on the inside. "I'm baptizing you here in the river, turning your old life in for a kingdom life. His baptism—a holy baptism by the Holy Spirit—will change you from the inside out" (Mk. 1:7-8 MSG). This outward act proclaims to the world that we're ready to leave behind the emphasis on this old body and move ahead with our new life in Christ.

GOD HELPS US CROSS THE FINISH LINE

During a track event, the anticipated winner approached the finish line. When he pulled a ligament in his leg, he stumbled and fell to the ground. His father rushed from the stands, picked him up, and with his arm around his son, helped him stumble across the finish line. Our Heavenly Father is committed to this kind of support and is anxious to assure us we can finish the race. His strong arms are available to lift us if we should fall on the way to the top. We're committed to go for the gold!

The Lord will not abandon us as we near the end of the journey. He started it all by offering the sacrifice of His Son, to put us on the right path for a saving relationship with Him. He has made every provision for us to be able to cross the finish line—safely home. God formulated a plan for us before our great-grandmas were born.

We've found that aging is not a time to cope, but a time to hope. "Relax, everything is going to be all right; everything is coming together; open your hearts, love is on its way" (Jude 1:2 MSG). God's wisdom is expressed in love. He gives rhyme and reason to everything that happens in the process of growing old.

So, it's time to spend less time in our rocking chairs. We've been rocking back and forth long enough—keeping ourselves busy, but not getting anywhere. We'll walk away from endless computer games. It will be no problem to shut off the television for a spell and make our greatest impact on the world. We'll delve into the truths of God's wisdom and find meaning in this transformation. We'll go with gusto, no turning back. This is no time to procrastinate. God's grace offers us a window of time for us to respond to His call. It's our opportunity to seize the day!

We find purpose in the aging process, a time of refinement as we release the grip on this world and submit to the will and purpose of God. We embrace the maladies of aging and the wasting away of this outer shell as we understand the resplendent beauty of an immortal spirit that has been developing within. Like the wise virgins waiting for the bridegroom, we fill our lamps with the oil of the Spirit. We'll keep them burning bright and held high until the door is opened. We want to provide light for others to follow.

Though we grow old and weary, we'll never give up. We stand firm with the declaration, "So we're not giving up. How could we! Even though on the outside it often looks like things are falling apart on us, on the inside, where God is creating a new life, not a day goes by without his unfolding grace… the things we can't see now will last forever" (2 Cor. 4:16 MSG).

The Holy Spirit has been acting as dialysis to extract the impurities from our souls as He constantly cleanses us from the inside out. God sent a fisher of men to reel us in, but then He sent the Holy Spirit to clean us up. I've decided to make a concerted effort to allow Him to deal with every secret sin of my life, saying, "Lord, expose and deal with sin now, rather than later!" Being clean on the inside, He's prepared to fill us with His love—a love that allows no room for sin or regret.

§

Stories are told of rich families in Europe fleeing from the enemy during World War II. They loaded silver, jewelry and expensive items in bags and lugged them along the road. As the days grew long and exhaustion wore them out they began to toss these expensive items in the ditches, retaining only food and necessary clothing to survive. We too find we've carried baggage that has no lasting value. It has slowed us down and hampered our progress.

Habits and hang-ups stick like ticks, but we're ready to pick them off before they suck life from our souls. The Christ in us shows us how to be persistent in plucking them off and casting them aside.

Look up. We should be nearing the peak, where we can look back with the same excitement the apostle Paul had when he shouted, "I have fought the good fight, I have finished the race, I have kept the faith. Now there is in store for me the crown of righteousness, which the Lord, the righteous Judge, will award to me on that day—and not only to me, but also to all who have longed for his appearing" (2 Tim. 4:7-8 NIV).

We've found God has had purpose in our aging. Our challenge is to ask the Father to reveal what He wants to teach us each step of the way. The total purpose of our struggles will not be revealed until we stand before the Great White Throne. We pray we brought glory to Him while here on earth, because we completed the work He laid out for us to do.

When the time comes for us to shed these earthly tents, we'll realize we've been away from our real home. Perhaps there won't be yellow ribbons flying from the Tree of Life, but we anticipate a glorious welcome from those who've gone ahead—those who are waiting and watching. We look forward to moving back home with our Father to live under His perfect rule. Our citizenship in heaven has been confirmed and we wait for our rite of passage.

Jesus will be our escort to take us with Him. He will transform these weak and worn-out bodies and change them into glorious immortal bodies like His own. The power that raised Jesus from the dead will also raise us up. In contrast to Dorothy in the Wizard of Oz, we'll not walk on a yellow brick road, but on streets of pure gold. But we will declare with her, "There's no place like home."

Nothing matters more at this stage of the game than finding out how God wants to put the finishing touches on the spirit residing within. It's all in preparation for the new kingdom we plan to live in. The time on the potter's wheel is almost over. We're ready to be placed in the kiln for the last time. It will reveal brilliant colors our Creator painted with His artistic touch.

The end of the world will come as a bolt of lightning! The galaxies will explode and the elements will melt on that final day. But while the world is thrown into panic, we'll watch in awesome wonder, anticipating the glorious new heaven and new earth, which will be landscaped with the righteousness of God. All the thorns and thistles of sin will be burned up.

The earth will shudder, the stars explode and God's thundering voice will reverberate throughout the whole universe. Those who have never bowed in submission to God will drop to their knees at the name of Jesus. Self-sufficiency will vanish. How terrible to face this moment with a lack of preparation, because one doesn't know the Lord. "Some of these people have missed the most important thing in life. They don't know God" (1 Tim. 6:21 LB).

Hearing will be no problem when that last trumpet sounds— no greater proclamation has ever called the world to stand at attention. It will be the final reveille that wakes the dead. Not only will we hear the blast of the trumpet, but Jesus will call his own,

"Come, you who are blessed by my Father, take your inheritance, the kingdom prepared for you since the creation of the world." (Matt. 25:34 NIV). How awesome to discover all things become new. There will be a new heaven, a new earth, a new body, a new home—none of which will ever grow old!

At that time, the curtain will be pulled back to reveal mysteries hidden from the foundation of the world. Revelations of the meaning of life will break forth in the presence of Truth. No doubt there will be a million 'Ah ha' experiences when we see the purpose of every trial, every test we've gone through. But it is just as the Scriptures say, "What God has planned for people who love him is more than eyes have seen or ears have heard. It has never even entered our minds!" (1 Cor. 2:9 CEV)

NOT GOOD-BYE—BUT SO LONG

As we stand beside a dying loved one, God can give us words of encouragement: "Go with God, my friend. I will miss you terribly. But one thing I know, it won't be long. Never again will we be separated by distance, but closer than sitting next to each other on the patio or the living room couch with a cup of coffee. It's time for me to turn loose of you, but we're committed to never turn loose of God. I loved you, and I will love you as my forever friend. The best has been saved until last."

I'll return that metal detector I borrowed in the beginning. The treasure hunt is over. I found my pot of gold at the end of the rainbow of God's promises. Indeed, this has proven to be the golden years. I FOUND **GOLD** WHILE **GROWING OLD.**

THINGS TO CONSIDER

1. In the end, what will count as the most meaningful thing in your life?

2. Are you aware that God is willing to do everything you allow Him to—to help you cross the finish line in victory?

3. Are you ready to praise God for planning to accomplish His great purpose in your life?

4. How can the wisdom you learned be passed on to others?

5. Do you see how God is using a refining process in your life?

6. How do you move from coping to hoping?

7. Are you determined to hold on to God until you finish your life here?

8. Are you dealing with habits and hang-ups that stand in the way with your relationship with God and others?

9. How do you plan to meet further challenges that come in your life?

10. Remember that this is the final exam and you come through Summa Cum Laude when you maintain a good attitude and hold steady with whatever life hands you.

ABOUT THE AUTHOR

Louise Looney conducts two Bible classes a week, facilitates a support group and is sought after as a public speaker. For the past number of years she has traveled to a Communist country for short periods of time to teach in an underground Bible training school. She taught in elementary school through college and in the prison system and worked as an educational diagnostician.

She worked as the Director of Spiritual Affairs in a psychiatric hospital and served as the Manager of a Christian Retreat center for 15 years.

Louise is available for speaking engagements. Her books may be ordered from her website with paypal. Postage is free. Her Web Site is: **LouiseLLooney.com.** She may also be reached by writing **LouiseLLooney@yahoo.com.**